ACTION!

Nothing Happens Until You Take
ACTION!

Robert Ringer

Skyhorse Publishing

Skyhorse Publishing books may be purchased in bulk at special discounts for sales promotion, corporate gifts, fund-raising, or educational purposes. Special editions can also be created to specifications. For details, contact the Special Sales Department, Skyhorse Publishing, 307 West 36th Street, 11th Floor, New York, NY 10018 or info@skyhorsepublishing.com.

Skyhorse® and Skyhorse Publishing® are registered trademarks of Skyhorse Publishing, Inc.®, a Delaware corporation.

Visit our website at www.skyhorsepublishing.com.

10 9 8 7 6 5 4 3 2

Library of Congress Cataloging-in-Publication Data is available on file.

Cover design by Owen Corrigan

ISBN: 978-1-62914-329-3

Printed in the United States of America

To My Family

Contents

Introduction

OVER THE PAST DECADE, I have become increasingly and consciously aware of a remarkable tool that is not only at my disposal, but is available to every member of the human species. It isn't that I was not previously familiar with this tool; on the contrary, I have employed it quite effectively throughout my adult life. What has changed is my heightened awareness of its preeminent role in steering the course of events.

The tool I am referring to is *action.* Its supreme position in the universal scheme of things—and, on a purely secular basis, in determining to what extent human beings succeed or fail—did not come to me as a sudden revelation. Rather, it was an accelerating evolution. Further, I am convinced that it is still evolving today. What I believe triggered my mind to begin focusing on action as the key ingredient in a meaningful life is a quote I happened to run across by the nineteenth-century German playwright, Johann Wolfgang von Goethe. Said von Goethe, "Boldness has genius, power, and magic in it." (I will be dissecting this quote in detail in Chapter 1.)

Goethe's words had such a dramatic impact on my thinking that they inspired me to go back and review my earlier self-development books in search of the word *action.* What I found is that each of those books is filled with anecdotes and stories about action, but the idea that action is the very essence of life is not addressed.

Today, I am absolutely convinced that neither success nor happiness is possible without action. Further, I firmly believe there is a direct link between action and spirituality. These conclusions are not based nearly so much on what I've read about action, but on firsthand experience. My increased understanding of the importance of action has resulted in a dramatically expanded insight into how life works and has given deeper meaning to my personal philosophical beliefs.

Cliché as it may be, writing this book was a true labor of love, and the reason for it became obvious to me early on. Clearly, it was because the book was based not only on what I most often speak about in public appearances, but on the way I live my life on a daily basis. Thus, with the publication of *Action!* my thinking, living, writing, and speaking are almost perfectly aligned.

Normally, the last words of a book bring feelings of relief and exhaustion. With *Action!* however, writing it was such a joy that it was the first time I can recall not wanting to see a book project come to an end. Hopefully, you will feel the same way when you finish reading it.

ON A SEPARATE NOTE, you will find a somewhat self-deprecating character known as "The Tortoise" popping up in a number of illustrations on the pages ahead. The Tortoise entered the world through my first book, *Winning through Intimidation*. I adopted him as my alter ego, so to speak, because so many of the anecdotes in that book were reminiscent of the legendary tortoise and hare tale.

The Tortoise is the classic antihero, the unglamorous plodder who always seems to find a way to come out ahead no matter how harshly life treats him along the way. Flash isn't his stock in trade; his strengths are consistency, perseverance, resiliency, and resourcefulness. He's the kind of reptile who, upon being told that he can't play in someone's game, simply goes out and starts his own league.

Above all, The Tortoise demonstrates that the outcome of most situations in life are decided over the long term. Quickly getting out of the starting blocks may get people's attention, but all that counts is where you are when the race is over.

CHAPTER 1

The Action Phenomenon

Twenty years from now you will be more disappointed by the things that you didn't do than by the ones you did do.

— MARK TWAIN

I HAVE ALWAYS BELIEVED that the difference between success and failure—in any area of life—is not nearly as great as most people might suspect. I have also been consistent in my belief that the slight difference between the two is primarily a result of whether or not one practices certain success "habits" that are based on universal wisdom, or, in simpler terms, *common sense.*

As the years have passed, however, I have increasingly zeroed in on action as *the most important* success habit when it comes to determining how an individual's life plays out. This life-changing conclusion evolved as a result of four key elements that gradually fit together in my mind like pieces of a jigsaw puzzle. These elements, which I think of as success pillars, work in concert with one another to make action an awesome tool that gives a person the capacity to overcome virtually any obstacle in his* path.

PILLAR NO. 1: NOTHING HAPPENS UNTIL SOMETHING MOVES

"Nothing happens until something moves" are the words of the greatest scientific mind of the twentieth century, Albert Einstein. The Theory of Relativity may have been Einstein's most important contribution to science, but these five simple words—"nothing happens until something moves"—comprise his most important contribution to *me*.

While his observation is an indisputable scientific fact, there is no doubt in my mind that it applies to all other aspects of life as well. Ideas can be precious commodities that can change the world; sound preparation is invaluable; and knowledge and wisdom are essential when it comes to giving one an edge in the pursuit of great achievements. But ideas, preparation, knowledge, and wisdom are all but useless without action, because action is the starting point of all progress.

In other words, an idea, of and by itself, has no intrinsic value. It must be accompanied by action. It is action that cuts the umbilical cord and brings an idea out of the womb. I can assure you that Fred Smith, founder of Federal Express, wasn't the only person to come up with the idea of starting an overnight delivery service to compete with the woefully incompetent U.S. Postal Service. The reason I can make such an assurance is that I myself thought about the concept for years, especially whenever I would have to send a secretary cross-country to hand deliver a document that needed to be in someone's office the next morning.

---

* Because I find it cumbersome to use hybrid pronouns such as "his/hers," and am opposed to debasing the English language by mixing singular nouns and pronouns with plural pronouns such as "they," I have, for the sake of convenience only, chosen to use the masculine gender throughout this book in most instances where the neuter has not been employed.

Further, I do not for a second believe I was the only other person to ponder the idea of an overnight mail-delivery service. In fact, I would be surprised if literally thousands of other entrepreneurs weren't simultaneously mulling over the same idea at the same time. What made Fred Smith different from the rest of us was that he didn't just think about the idea; he took *action*. Action converts an idea into an experience. Action creates reality. In Fred Smith's case, he brought his college thesis on the subject to life by applying action to his written words.

The same story has been repeated thousands of times through the years. To give a more recent example, I doubt Jeff Bezos was the first person to envision a business like Amazon.com, one of the biggest companies ever built in such a short period of time. Talk about a simple idea. What could be more simple, more obvious, and more dull than selling books on the Internet?

And once he got started, Bezos did not allow a little problem like not turning a profit for many years slow him down. Instead, he kept taking action on two fronts: increasing Amazon.com's greatest asset—its customer base—and repeatedly convincing Wall Street to invest more millions of dollars in that asset. If you've ever tried to raise additional capital for a money-losing venture, you can appreciate the enormity of Bezos's feat—and it's a feat he has repeatedly accomplished.

As a final example, I recall some years back watching what appeared to be a rather uninspiring interview with singer/songwriter Paul Simon of Simon and Garfunkel fame. Simon had just come out with a new album based on the tribal sounds of Africa. The interviewer asked Simon how he felt about the pounding he had been taking from critics in the industry whose position was that "anybody could have taken existing African sounds and packaged them into an album."

His bland response to the interviewer's question was, "Maybe it's true that anyone *could* have done it, but I *did* it." On the surface, Simon's retort seemed to be rather unremarkable, but it certainly caught my attention. I may be the only person in the world who remembers that uneventful interview, but it had such a huge impact on my thinking that I've quoted Simon's response scores of times over the years. The moral is self-evident: It's not what you *can* do; it's what you *do* that counts.

Nolan Bushnell, founder of Atari, Inc., put it bluntly when he said, "The critical ingredient is getting off your butt and doing something. It's as simple as that. A lot of people have ideas, but there are few who decide to do something about them now. Not tomorrow. Not next week. But today. The true entrepreneur is a doer, not a dreamer."

As I have narrowed my focus to the phenomenon of action, it has become ever more apparent to me that the very essence of life is action. Inertia—resistance to action—is antilife. Except in horror films, corpses tend to be extremely inactive.

I don't recall where I first heard the following parable, but it certainly is profound and appropriate to any discussion about the importance of action.

> *Every morning in Africa, a gazelle wakes up. It knows that it must run faster than the fastest lion or it will be killed.*
>
> *Every morning in Africa, a lion wakes up. It knows that it must run faster than the slowest gazelle or it will starve.*
>
> *It doesn't matter whether you're a lion or a gazelle; when the sun comes up, you had better start running.*

As human beings, we find that we, too, had better start running at the crack of dawn if we're serious about making life a meaningful journey. A stress-free life sounds nice in theory, but, in reality, there is an inherent urgency to life. For one thing, life is finite, and you don't even have the advantage of knowing when your finite supply of time will run out. Second, life is competition. No matter what the situation, you're always competing with other human beings. You compete for a prospective spouse, you compete for a place on an athletic team, you compete for attention from others, you constantly compete in numerous ways that you don't even think about.

If you don't want the competition to leave you in the dust, you can't coast. You've got to take positive action and make progress every day of your life.

THE BEST DAY IS TODAY

There are two basic kinds of actions. One is *proaction*, which puts you on the offensive and, all other things being equal, gives you a great deal of control over events. The other is *reaction*, which puts you on the defensive and relegates you to a position of weakness.

An interesting way of looking at inaction is that it's really just a negative form of action—a sort of black hole of action that sucks energy away from you much the same as the black holes of the universe pull matter into the deep recesses of their cosmic bowels. This is why inaction often yields consequences by default. Nothing happens until something moves, so if you wait for something, or someone, to act *on* you, you are unlikely to be unable to control the consequences.

Homeostasis, a trait that all human beings possess to one extent or another, is (in psychological terms) the tendency to live with existing conditions and avoid change. Which is ironic, because resistance to change defies both the laws of nature and the laws of the universe. The earth, the universe, and life itself are in a perpetual state of change, and so, too, is secular life. In addition, with the generation and dying of cells in our bodies, each of us is in a constant state of change physiologically, from birth to death.

Homeostasis is the ultimate defense against taking action, which is why most people stubbornly resist change, particularly major change. Outwardly, of course, we fabricate excuses that attempt to justify why we aren't able to take action just yet, the most common one being that "the time is not quite right." Someday, we insist, when all the pieces of our lives fit perfectly together, we'll be in a better position to take action—change occupations, go back to school and get an engineering degree, get out of a bad marriage, start working on that big project we've thought about for years, move to the city of our dreams, or begin writing the novel that we've always believed would be a bestseller.

But it's all delusion. The truth of the matter is that, with few exceptions, the best day to take action is today. You *can* make a sales call today. You *can* start working on that important project today. You *can* begin to pick up the pieces and start a new life today. The issue isn't about today being the first day of the rest of your life. The real issue is that today could be the *last* day of the rest of your life!

When people cling to the excuse that the time isn't quite right to move forward with a plan or change of one kind or another, it's often because they get caught up in the "how" of the situation. No one is omniscient. No one can foresee every problem and know, in advance, how to resolve it. The reality is that all start-ups are dysfunctional. What makes a person an entrepreneur is that he has the determination, perseverance, and resourcefulness to overcome the dysfunction of a new enterprise. Paul McCartney put it well when asked in an interview how the Beatles got started. Said McCartney, "Nobody knows how to do it. You just start a band."

In the same vein, people often fail to take action because they confuse the word *hard* with *impossible*. The fact that most worthwhile objectives are hard is what gives them their value. *Everything* worth accomplishing is hard.

If you're waiting for everything to be just right before taking action, you're likely to wait your entire life. Don't fear change; embrace it as one of the most exciting aspects of life. Think of action as an opportunity to make mistakes, mistakes that give you a front-row seat in the Theater of Learning. Carlos Castañeda explained it succinctly when he said, "A warrior lives by acting, not by thinking about acting, nor by thinking about what he will think when he has finished acting."

When it comes to having the courage to make a major change in one's life, my memory takes me back many years ago to a chance meeting in Palm Springs, California, where a friend and I happened to stop in at a hotel lounge one evening. Without fanfare, the act for the lounge was introduced—a stunningly beautiful female singer ("Dionne").

She bore a striking resemblance to the legendary Lena Horne, and carried herself with the style and grace of royalty. From the moment she began singing, patrons in the small lounge were mesmerized. In this unlikely venue, Dionne received numerous standing ovations, including several encores. I had never seen anything quite like it. There was no question in my mind that I was witnessing the birth of a star.

After finishing her act, Dionne sat at a table and chatted with some acquaintances. Being the young and impetuous tortoise I was, I scribbled a note to her on the back of my business card, asking whether she had a manager, then had a waiter deliver the card to her. To my pleasant surprise, she sent back a note saying that she, in fact, did not have a manager. After a couple more notes back and forth, I set up an appointment for Dionne to meet with me in my office later in the week.

Our initial meeting went well and, after a couple weeks of negotiations, I succeeded in signing her to a management contact. Among other things, the contract called for me to finance a demo tape, arrange for the production of an album, and use my marketing skills to promote her talents. In the course of filling out a variety of forms, Dionne told me she was thirty-two years old, which surprised me, because I had guessed her age at about twenty-seven or twenty-eight. I wondered why someone with her beauty, presence, and, above all, extraordinary talent was not already a household name by age thirty-two.

Dionne explained to me that she had studied classical music in college but had not pursued a career, opting instead for marriage and the life of a traditional housewife. She described the hunger she had felt inside her for so many years, believing that her purpose in life was far different from the way things had unfolded for her up to that point in time. She realized that she had been given a gift at birth, and a little voice from within kept telling her that it was wrong not to use that gift. Finally, one day, she made up her mind to take bold action to change her circumstances, and thus began her belated singing career.

But the most impressive thing Dionne said to me was in response to my warnings about how tough the music business was and how fickle and unpredictable the public could be. In a characteristic-ally self-confident manner, she smiled and told me that if she never became famous—if she was relegated to playing in small lounges the rest of her life—it wouldn't matter to her, because she was doing what she loved. The stage, no matter how small, was her world, and an appreciative audience, no matter how sparse, her reward. I was super impressed with her purist attitude and her passion for performing.

As things progressed—cutting a demo tape, making an appearance on a national talk show, and preparing for an album—it occurred to me that, considering the large investment I was making in Dionne, I had better take out a life-insurance policy on her. When I explained that she would have to take a physical exam, she wavered a bit, but, because it was called for in our contract, she had no choice. However, when it came time to fill out the insurance application form, she asked if she could first speak with me in private, so we set up a time for her to come to my office.

When Dionne walked through the door, she brought along a surprise—two surprises, in fact. Make that two *very tall* surprises. I assumed that one of the twin towers was her boyfriend and the other his acquaintance, so when she introduced them to me as her *sons*, I nervously chuckled and waited for a more serious introduction. Alas, her first introduction *was* a serious introduction. Stunned, I asked everyone to sit down and enlighten me as to what this was all about.

Almost everything Dionne had told me was true—her study of classical music in college, initially playing the role of the traditional housewife, then pursuing her destiny as a singer, and the fact that she had no manager. The part of the story that had not been true, however, was her age. Given that I had thought she looked younger than the thirty-two years of age she admitted to, it would be an understatement to say that I was not prepared to hear her *real* age. Knowing that she was required to put her age on the insurance application, Dionne had decided she would first break the news to me in person. As it turned out, she was not thirty-two, and certainly not in her late twenties as I had originally supposed. Dionne was *forty-seven years old*—a female Peter Pan! Put another way, she was a medical miracle.

After the paramedics revived me, Dionne, her twin-tower sons, and I had a warm chat, saturated, as you might have imagined, with a number of humorous one-liners about her age. The twin towers particularly liked my tongue-in-cheek barb about taking mom on the road and making a fortune by having people place wagers on her age. I suggested that if we got started right away, we could all be rich before Dionne was confined to a nursing home.

"And now, I give you my latest and greatest discovery—
the young, the beautiful, the exciting . . . Dionne!"

As things turned out, my relationship with Dionne lasted only about a year, chiefly because I couldn't afford to continue the level of investment I felt was required. The music business gives new meaning to the term *dirty*, and it became apparent that, despite Dionne's talent, it was going to be a long, hard road to the top—and long was something that was in very short supply in her case.

9

When we parted ways, Dionne reaffirmed her feelings that even if she never became famous, she would be more than satisfied just doing what she loved. I haven't seen her in more than twenty-five years, and the thought that she is now nearly seventy-five years old is unfathomable to me. And so, too, is the thought that she may even look almost forty by now.

Dionne knew in her heart what was right for her, but I believe that's true of most people. What made her unusual was that, notwithstanding her age, she had the mental toughness to *take action* to change the course of her life. She made a shambles of the overused excuse of millions of people who insist that it's too late for them to make major changes in their lives. I would be surprised if she isn't still on stage, still smiling, still knocking 'em dead, still getting regular standing ovations in small lounges across the country.

Dionne's bold action should be an inspiration to those who make the mistake of playing it close to the vest and waiting for something to happen. If you want something to happen, *make* it happen! You don't have to wait for the perfect pitch in the hopes of hitting a grand-slam home run. Grand-slam home runs don't come along very often. Striking out swinging is a noble action; striking out with the bat on your shoulder represents a pathetic lack of action. Take more swings at pitches that aren't perfect and get your share of singles and doubles every day. Singles and doubles make it possible for you to still be at bat when that perfect pitch finally arrives. Then, if you're prepared, you'll be in a position to hit one out of the park.

The formula is quite simple: The more action you take, the more results you get. Remember, nothing happens until something moves.

PILLAR NO. 2: GOD HELPS THOSE WHO HELP THEMSELVES

To discuss the concept of God is a precarious endeavor, at best. Since so many people have such strong views on the subject, it is guaranteed to cause a lot of anger. Let's face it, a significant percentage of the world's population is not rational when it comes to discussing the possibility of a Creator.

Fundamentalism, in the generic sense, is the strict adherence to a set of ideas, and is, by definition, at odds with objectivity. This is true whether it be fundamentalist Christianity, fundamentalist Islam, or fundamentalist atheism. All too often, fundamentalists begin their arguments by masking their conclusions as premises. For example, if someone starts with the premise that the Bible is the word of God, or, in the alternative, starts with the premise that there is no God, his premise is, in reality, a personal conclusion (his conclusion). The fact that he feels the need to disguise his own conclusion as a premise merely demonstrates a lack of belief. God—if He exists—is certainly powerful enough to withstand serious investigation.

Though I am well aware that to begin to do justice to this, the most important of all of life's questions, would take a thousand pages and a lifetime of research, I ask that you indulge me as I attempt, as a layman, to abridge my own thoughts in a matter of a few pages. For our purposes here—i.e., to explain why I believe that "God helps those who help themselves"—there are a number of possibilities with regard to the existence or nonexistence of God that deserve to be addressed.

QUIETISM

Quietism is the most gruesome way of viewing the universe. It is the belief that the past, present, and future are all illusions of our consciousness, and that, in reality, they are one and the same. In this view of the universe, nothing can be changed, either by God or man; everything is permanent. If so, there is no reason to try to improve your life, because there is no future. Since quietism gives us a universe where everything is already in place, the universe is, in effect, dead.

As a philosophy, however, quietism is a moot point. If all of life is but an illusion, we may as well try to be the best we can and reach for the highest goals possible. After all, if we're really just part of a cosmic dream, we'll never know it for certain anyway. However, in the (likely) event that quietism is not an accurate portrayal of the universe, those who live life on the assumption that secular events are real, and that what they accomplish matters, are certain to be far better off than those who believe that life is nothing more than an illusion.

ATHEISTIC RANDOMNESS

Most atheists believe that we live in a random universe. On closer inspection, however, we find that the term *randomness* is really a misnomer. It would be more appropriate to call it "atheistic predestination," "atheistic fatalism," or simply "predestined chaos."

Why? Because the atheistic-randomness advocate generally believes that the so-called Big Bang—the massive explosion from whence evolved today's known universe—somehow happened without the aid of a Supreme Power. And if there was, and is, no Supreme Power in the universe, everything that has been, is, or will be said and done throughout world history was precisely determined approximately 14 billion years ago by the nature of the Big Bang.

At the first instant of that colossal explosion, every atom began an eternal voyage that was predetermined by the nature of the explosion. If there is no Supreme Power to intervene, then nothing can be changed by anybody or anything. Every detail of every event has already been set on an unalterable course. It is the ultimate fatalistic view of the universe. There is no one in control, and there is no purpose to life.

Purists of the philosophy of atheistic predestination believe that if you say, "But I can make a conscious decision right now to buy tickets to the Yankee game today," not only is your free will to make such a decision an illusion, but so, too, is your belief that you *think* you are acting out of free will; i.e., even your perception that you are making a decision to buy baseball tickets was predetermined 14 billion years ago. That's because the Big Bang propelled into the universe the atoms that formed your brain in such a way that it would *think* it was making the decision to purchase baseball tickets today.

In short, atheistic predestination is the most extreme form of fatalism. Not only can nothing be changed, but everything has already been decided. However, as with quietism, the question of atheistic predestination is a moot point. If everything has already been decided, we will never know it for certain anyway. So, again, we may as well go ahead with pursuing our secular goals, and, in our blissful ignorance, keep right on believing that they're important. But if atheistic predestination turns out to be incorrect, when the end comes you don't want to be caught scratching your head in disbelief while those around you have been taking action all their lives.

DIVINE FATALISM

Divine fatalism, or divine predestination, is the belief that some or all of the future has already been determined by a Divine Power. If that Power caused the Big Bang, but has not intervened and does not intend to intervene beyond His initial act, then we might properly refer to Him as the Cosmic Designer. This leaves us with a pilot-less universe that appears in many respects to operate in a precise fashion, but in other ways appears to be as random as the atheist's fatalistic universe.

One could speculate that the results of the Cosmic Designer's predestined universe would be the same as if the Big Bang happened by itself, which, in turn, would lead one to wonder why He would bother to create the universe in the first place. Regardless, in either fatalistic scenario, the course of events has already been determined, which renders man impotent. Thus, while events may seem random, in reality they have been predetermined by an outside force, either God or a massive, mindless explosion.

However, if God not only designed the universe (either by virtue of the Big Bang or by some other means with which we are not familiar), but remains at the controls and intervenes in secular life, it might be more appropriate to refer to him as the Cosmic Pilot. A Cosmic Designer doesn't make house calls; he just sits back and observes his creation. A Cosmic Pilot stays on top of things. So, whether God set everything in stone at the outset or is still at the steering wheel is of monumental importance in our lives.

Since we can never prove which scenario is correct, again it would seem rational for one to forge ahead with pursuing his goals through an action-oriented life.

HUMANISTIC SELF-DETERMINATION

As with fatalism, there is both an atheistic and a divine version of self-determination. The atheist's version encompasses the belief that human beings are in total control of their destiny, and that man reigns supreme. I do not reject this belief on religious grounds. I reject it on the basis of firsthand experience, logic, and fact.

Humanists believe that science invalidates God, in that God becomes irrelevant in the face of scientific explanations of the nature of the universe. But does He? Increasingly, a growing number of astronomers and space physicists seem to be expressing doubts about a random universe.

For example, science can explain *how* gravity works, but it cannot explain *why* it works the way it does. We know that gravity makes the planets, stars, galaxies, and other cosmic bodies act on each other in certain predictable ways, but this does nothing to explain how the principle of gravity came into being. Similarly, scientists know *how* molecular formation works (e.g., under the right conditions, two atoms of hydrogen will always combine with one atom of oxygen to form a molecule of water), but they don't know *why* it works the way it does. They know *how* wind works, but they don't know *why* it works the way it does. And so on.

In his book *God and the Astronomers*, Robert Jastrow, founder of NASA's Goddard Institute for Space Studies, put it this way: "For the scientist who has lived by his faith in the power of reason, the story ends like a bad dream. He has scaled the mountains of ignorance; he is about to conquer the highest peak; as he pulls himself over the final rock, he is greeted by a band of theologians who have been sitting there for centuries."

Clearly, the chasm between theologians and scientists seems to be narrowing toward a middle-ground belief that science is not in conflict with God, but, rather, is a gift of God. Consider, for example, evolution. Let us assume, for purposes of discussion, that evolution is not just a theory, but a fact. Does this invalidate God? No, on the contrary, quite the opposite. It provides strong mathematical support for the idea that there is a Supreme Power at the controls of the universe.

As Guy Murchie points out in his book *The Seven Mysteries of Life*, an intellectual, long-standing argument for a random universe wherein a seeming miracle such as evolution could take place on its own is that, given enough time, anything—including the evolution of human beings from inanimate matter—is possible. This argument, says Murchie, is based on the premise that if you could sit enough billions of chimpanzees in front of computers for enough billions of years, random chance would allow them to write all the great works of literature.

Which sounds nice until you consider the mathematics involved. There are approximately fifty possible letters, numbers, and punctuation marks on a computer keyboard, and there are sixty-five character spaces per line in the average book. A chimp would therefore have a one in fifty chance of getting the first space on the first line correct. Since the same is true of the second space on that line, the chimp would have one chance in 50 x 50, or 50^2, of getting both spaces right (meaning just the first two letters of the first word of just *one* of the great works of literature). For all sixty-five spaces on the first line, the figure would jump to 50^{65}, which is equal to 10^{110}.

How big is 10^{110}? According to physicist George Gamow, says Murchie, it is a thousand times greater than the total number of vibrations made by all the atoms in the universe since the Big Bang!

Conclusion: It doesn't matter how many chimpanzees or how much time you allow, not even one line of one great work could come into existence through pure chance. Given that you are infinitely more complex than one line of a book, what are the odds that you, with all your billions of precise, specialized cells, accidentally evolved from rocks and dirt over a period of a few billion years? Evolution in a random universe—i.e., a universe without a Cosmic Pilot—would appear to be a mathematical impossibility. As with wind and gravity, it would seem that the only way that a phenomenon such as evolution could have come into existence is through the work of a Supreme Power that is beyond secular comprehension.

SELF-DETERMINATION AND THE COSMIC CATALYST

As the years have passed, I have become increasingly impressed with two phenomena. The first is the remarkable capacity I possess to determine the outcome of my life. For those of us who are not humanists, our secular consciousness (which includes our ability to observe and interpret both history and our own experiences) clearly suggests that we are able to exert a considerable amount of control over our destiny.

The second phenomenon is the outside forces that always seem to come into play whenever I take action. The bolder my action, the more powerful those outside forces seem to be. If man has the power to play a major role in controlling his own destiny, logic would dictate that he also has to have a power *source*.

Secularly speaking, most people refer to this power source as "God," "Allah," "Yahweh," and a variety of other names that are language based. You could just as well refer to it as the Big Guy in the Sky, and it would not change what He is or what He does. Because I have no secular explanation for this power source, I choose to refer to it as the *Cosmic Catalyst*. This is just another language-based way of describing what I perceive to be His relationship to human action.

Though I believe the Cosmic Catalyst is also the Cosmic Designer and Cosmic Pilot (i.e., for reasons we do not fully understand, He intervenes), on a day-to-day secular level I see Him as the catalyst that precipitates results from our actions. In this view, the Cosmic Catalyst designs, then stays on the job at the controls. What it gets down to, then, is a combination of predestination and self-determination. The Cosmic Catalyst predetermines some or most events, but not all.

And because man possesses free will, he can make choices that alter those events that are not totally controlled by the Cosmic Catalyst. Religionists refer to this ability of man as "free will," and the debate over this concept will surely continue until mankind ceases to exist. It is one of the greatest mysteries of life, yet its existence—at least from a secular point of view—seems self-evident.

The question that the middle-ground position of self-determination and predestination (and/or divine intervention) leaves eternally unanswered is: If the Cosmic Designer/Pilot predetermines some events and intervenes in others, which events are left for man to alter? It is this unanswered question that makes it sound like a contradiction when a self-reliant, positive person makes a statement such as, "If it's meant to be, it's meant to be."

For purposes of this book, the subject of fatalism versus self-determination constitutes far more than just an interesting intellectual discussion. It gets at the very heart of the justification for taking action. If you believe that only some things are predetermined, I would suggest that you not spend a lot of time worrying about which things are inevitable and which things are within your control. It makes a lot more sense to just pitch in and help the Cosmic Catalyst work His wonders—from whence comes the saying, "God helps those who help themselves."

In simple terms, "God helps those who help themselves" means that God helps those who take action. This is a predictable phenomenon, given that you are always connected to the Cosmic Catalyst. The reason you don't have to tap into His infinite powers is that you are permanently connected to Him from the time you are born. And because the Cosmic Catalyst has infinite power and knowledge, He can provide you with a solution to every problem—real or imagined—that you encounter.

You are undoubtedly familiar with the little parable about "footprints in the sand" wherein a man says to God (in a dream), "I don't understand why, when I needed you most, you have not been there for me." To which God replies, "The times when you have seen only one set of footprints is when I carried you." It is merely a poetic way of expressing that God is always standing by, ready to help. The only unknown is whether or not *you* are going to take action. The vast majority of the time, if you do your part, the Cosmic Catalyst will come through on His end.

PILLAR NO. 3: THE LAW OF AVERAGES

The Cosmic Catalyst has blessed us with a powerful universal principle that provides an accurate method for projecting results. The principle I am referring to is commonly known as the *Law of Averages*, and, like all other universal principles, it never fails to work. Further, it applies to every aspect of life—from finding a spouse to closing a sale to applying for college admission.

The Law of Averages itself is passive; i.e., it is not driven by action. It just sits invisibly in the background and operates impassively. Without outside action, it's nothing more than a mathematical tool.

Insurance companies use it to compile actuary tables, sports teams keep statistics on all phases of their games, and, of course, gambling casinos put the fate of their enterprises totally in the hands of the Law of Averages, which never fails them over the long term.

However, even though the Law of Averages itself is passive, you can use it to achieve your objectives by applying action to it. When you do so, it's guaranteed to come through for you *over the long term*. Put another way, because the Cosmic Catalyst helps those who help themselves, the more you help yourself (i.e., the more action you take), the more help you will get from the Cosmic Catalyst via the Law of Averages.

Everyone is familiar with Woody Allen's famous line that "90 percent of success is showing up." It may be a slight exaggeration, but his somewhat tongue-in-cheek observation strikes a chord in people. I find it absolutely fascinating how often good things happen to me when I do nothing more than "show up." Just landing on someone's doorstep can dramatically change a person's success equation. This is not to imply that you will succeed every time you show up, but showing up is the *first* step toward success. Keep in mind that nothing can happen until something moves, so it's nice to know that you are in control of whether or not you take that first step.

However, I would modify Woody Allen's observation and suggest that perhaps only 45 percent of success is showing up, while another 45 percent of success is asking. Asking is the simplest, most efficient, and potentially most rewarding action a person can take. I've become such a believer in the power of asking that I am compelled to share with you my Ten Sacred Rules of Success:

Rule No. 1:   Ask.
Rule No. 2:   Ask again.
Rule No. 3:   Ask again.
Rule No. 4:   Ask again.
Rule No. 5:   Ask again.
Rule No. 6:   Ask again.
Rule No. 7:   Ask again.
Rule No. 8:   Ask again.
Rule No. 9:   Ask again.
Rule No. 10:   Ask again.

I never cease to be amazed by how many times I've achieved results simply because I took the trouble (and, in many cases, had the gall or audacity) to ask—and kept asking until I got the *yes* I was after. As I have repeatedly told my employees over the years, if you aren't a *pain in the ask* to people who are lazy, negligent, and/or just love to say *no,* you aren't doing your job properly.

Don't get me wrong; asking does not work 100 percent of the time. The important thing about asking is that it works *in conjunction with* the Law of Averages. The Law of Averages makes time your ally instead of your enemy. Asking is an incredibly powerful tool, and even more powerful if you understand the importance of asking *again* . . . and *again* . . . and *again.*

CLOSING ONE OF THE most unlikely deals of my life came about as a direct result of (1) showing up and (2) asking. I was trying to raise $5 million for a software project I was working on, and, through my New York patent attorney, had made contact with a German investment banker who showed an interest in the project—enough interest to begin a long and expensive undertaking of having a prospectus drawn up for some of his clients.

(Before going further with this story, I should point out that I had long ago learned that it's always a bad idea to wait for funding before starting a project. If you believe in something, move forward with it—*take action*—as quickly as possible. One of the best-kept secrets of raising money is that funding is always easier when a project is already under way. Conversely, the easiest excuse in the world for never taking action is to wait for a project to be fully funded.)

It became obvious to me that it was going to be quite a while before the investment banker would be able to raise the $5 million, and I was nearing the point where I would be ready to do some test marketing. My subconscious mind had long been thinking about ways to get some quick marketing money in the till. Then, one day, during a telephone discussion with my New York attorney, he happened to mention that the investment banker was coming in from Germany the following week to meet with him on another matter. Unbeknownst to him, it was a call to action for me. I immediately decided

I would make arrangements to meet with the German banker while he was in New York.

My attorney thought it would be a terrible waste of my time and money to make the cross-country trip, assuring me that the investment banker would not be open to any further proposals until he finished the prospectus and presented it to his clients. I thanked him for his advice, but told him that I definitely would be making the trip to New York the following week anyway. I then called the investment banker and told him that I had a counterproposal I would like to discuss with him (even though I had *no specific proposal in mind* at the time), and *asked* if we could meet in my attorney's office when he came to the U.S. He agreed to do so, and an appointment time was set.

As I said, I didn't have a specific plan in mind; it was just those rapidly vibrating atoms in my brain subconsciously reminding me that nothing happens until something moves. The five-hour plane ride from the West Coast provided me with more than ample time to come up with several ideas to present to the investment banker. It's important to emphasize that I was not motivated to take the trip because I had already come up with one or more specific ideas; rather, I was motivated to come up with ideas *as a result of taking the trip*—a case of action *preceding* motivation!

The first proposal I made to the investment banker was the one I felt made the most sense from his standpoint. I told him I would be willing to take one-tenth of the $5 million ($500,000) just to be able to start test marketing the product if he would be willing to bypass the prospectus for now and come up with the money personally. Then, if things went well, he could take his time and raise the balance of the $5 million via the prospectus route. I emphasized that it was a great deal for him because he would be able to find out if the product was marketable before putting almost $4.5 million of his clients' money on the line.

The investment banker asked a handful of questions, then told me that he would like to talk the matter over in private with his associate, whereupon they excused themselves and went to a conference room down the hall. In about fifteen minutes they returned to my attorney's office, expressionless, and sat down. Without pause, and in a calm, straightforward manner, the investment banker said, "Okay, we'll go along with the proposal to put up the $500,000. Can you wait until Monday for a check?" I had to restrain myself from jumping up and shouting, "Yes!" In suave, tortoise-like fashion, however, I kept my composure, cleared my throat, and casually responded, "Sure. No problem."

When I received the $500,000 check, I recall thinking to myself that it never would have happened had I not taken the trouble to do two things: *show up* and *ask*. So much for listening to the advice of attorneys.

OF COURSE, NOT EVERY payoff that results from the mere act of asking is as big as the one I just described. Most, in fact, are on the small side. Nevertheless, when the payoffs come nearly every day of your life, they add up. One area where I've made it a habit to employ the simple act of asking is when I speak to customer-support-type people over the phone. When a company representative gives me a *no* to a request, I often thank him, hang up the phone, then immediately dial the number again and talk to another representative. More often than not, I end up getting a *yes* out of the second person I speak to.

So, time is on your side, provided you take continual action. It's pretty simple mathematics: If a salesman earns a nice living by making ten sales calls a day, the Law of Averages virtually assures him that he will make a nice living times two if he makes twenty sales calls a day.

That's the good news about time. The bad news is that without action, time becomes the casino in the game of life. If you hesitate or procrastinate, time will ultimately wipe you out. If the same hypothetical salesman instead makes only two sales calls a day, the Time Casino will break him. Think of it this way: If a salesman makes $1 million in a year, that's a lot of money. But if he makes $1 million over a forty-year career, that's an average of $25,000 a year—virtual poverty! Moral: Time matters when it comes to the Law of Averages. The Law of Averages will never fail to do its part, but *you* have to supply the action.

PILLAR NO. 4: ACTION PRODUCES GENIUS, MAGIC, AND POWER

The words of nineteenth-century German playwright Johann Wolfgang von Goethe, "Boldness has genius, power, and magic in it," have had a great impact on my life. For my personal use, I have modified von Goethe's words to read, "Action produces genius, magic, and power." Boldness implies action—and the bolder the action, the greater the genius, magic, and power that is likely to flow from it. You will note that I list power third in this sequence, the reason being that power is the culmination not only of action, but of the genius and magic that result from action.

There is something wondrous about action that is impossible to adequately describe. Action is the key to the brain's ignition. Contrary to popular belief, you don't need to be motivated to act. If necessary, *force* yourself to take action, and motivation will follow. It is the combination of action, genius, magic, and power that produces motivation, which, in turn, leads to ever more action.

Action stimulates both the body and brain cells. It brings you in contact with surprising things, unexpected events, and incredible people who have the potential to be crucial to your success. Take action *first*—even if it's just to explore possibilities—and your creative juices will rise to the occasion. And when that happens, you will become increasingly motivated to take still more action.

Because genius, magic, and power are unique and integral parts of the action equation, they merit individual discussion.

GENIUS

When it comes to the relationship between action and genius, some might view it as a chicken-and-egg situation. Does action produce genius or does genius produce action? I would say it's a positive cycle wherein both are true; i.e., as with motivation, action produces genius, and genius, in turn, inspires one to take more action. However, you have to come down on the side of action as the first cause—the initial spark that sets the positive cycle in motion. Action, in other words, brings out the genius in a person before genius returns the favor. Action is life. Action is energy. Remember, until something moves, nothing happens.

The genius I am referring to here has little to do with raw IQ. If anything, it is more closely related to "emotional intelligence." Emotional intelligence has to do with creative thinking that leads to tangible, real-world results, as opposed to intellectual thinking, which produces only academic results.

Action-generated genius results from a phenomenon I like to refer to as an "expansive mental paradigm"—i.e., the capacity to think beyond one's normal system of beliefs and tap into the infinite intelligence of the Cosmic Catalyst. I use the term *mental paradigm* to describe an imaginary box within your mind, a box that houses what you believe to be the world of the possible. Thus, everything that lies outside of this box is considered to be impossible to you. Your "system of beliefs" is pretty much made up of which things lie inside the box and which things lie outside.

What determines on which side of the box's boundaries something lies are your experiences, your education, your environment—everything you've been exposed to throughout your life that has helped to shape your belief system. When you expand your mental paradigm, your mind is open to new ideas, new concepts, and new possibilities. A rigid mental paradigm equates to a closed mind, similar to a dead universe where everything is already in place and nothing can be changed.

Today's hip corporate slang includes the expression "thinking outside the box," which is just another way of referring to an expansive mental paradigm. Unfortunately, most people who talk about thinking outside the box haven't a clue as to what it really means. Corporate types love to mouth the latest "in" jargon, but, as everyone in the business world is aware, the typical corporate atmosphere isn't known for encouraging people to stick their necks out and take bold action.

What's so exciting about a human being's capacity to expand his mental paradigm is that it gives him the power to *manipulate* the Law of Averages, i.e., improve his odds of succeeding. Human beings, unlike any other species, are much more than just conscious

Mental Paradigm

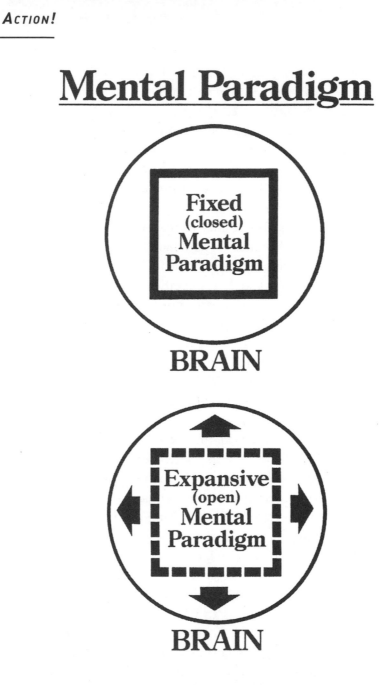

creatures. Perhaps the most significant difference between a man and an animal is that an animal knows, but a man knows that he knows.

An animal looks at the heavens and has no idea what he's looking at; a man not only has a scientific understanding of what he's looking at when he views the sky, but he also can *reflect* on what he sees. It's awesome to think about the fact that a human being is the only matter on our planet whose atoms are arranged in such a way that it can reflect on its very existence.

A human being can *choose* to change the nature of his existence by altering events, because he has the capacity to plot, plan, conceptualize, and even will things to happen. What this means is that a human being can choose to go beyond the bondage of his belief system and tap into the infinite intelligence of the Cosmic Catalyst. As William James observed, "The greatest revolution of our generation is the discovery that human beings, by changing the inner attitudes of their minds, can change the outer aspects of their lives."

An individual can make conscious decisions to smoke or not smoke, drive fast or slow, or eat healthy or unhealthy food. And each of his decisions can dramatically improve his chances when it comes to his health and longevity. He can also decide whether to get out of a bad marriage or love relationship, stay put or move to another city, and remain in his current job or start a new career. And each of these decisions can have a dramatic effect on how the remainder of his life plays out.

Another way of viewing an expansive mental paradigm is that it is the birthplace of resourcefulness, or "alternative thinking." By *alternative thinking*, I mean looking for alternative solutions *outside* of your normal belief system when confronted with seemingly impossible circumstances. The trick is to do this *in lieu of* focusing on the apparent impossibility of a situation.

Further, since we don't know all the possibilities that exist outside of our mental paradigms, theoretically speaking, our limitations are pretty much where we choose to place them. When you tap into this limitless reservoir of ideas and opportunities, it's important to understand that you may not always find a solution that allows you to achieve your original objective. Instead, you may find an alternative that takes you in an entirely different direction, but a direction that more often than not turns out to be superior to the one in which you were originally headed.

Perhaps the best way to define an expansive mental paradigm is to refer to it as a heightened state of awareness, an awareness that is unquestionably intensified by action. And the bolder the action, the more intense a person's awareness is. Of course, there are other kinds of actions than just body movement. Meditation is action, writing is action, reading is action. What a tragedy it would be to live eighty years and never get around to buying and reading *the book* that could have played a major role in your success. Anything you do, so long as it is purposeful and constructive, may be considered positive action, but, make no mistake about it, the greatest expansion of your mental paradigm comes from taking *bold* action.

What helped me gain a better understanding of the heightened state of awareness I have just referred to was a book I stumbled across some time ago, *Cosmic Consciousness,* by Dr. Richard Maurice Bucke, originally published in 1901. Dr. Bucke was a graduate of McGill Medical School and a prominent psychiatrist in Canada. Sadly, he died from an accidental fall on the ice, at age sixty-five, a year after his book was published.

At age thirty-six, Dr. Bucke experienced an "illumination" that lasted only a few seconds, but during which time he claimed to have learned more than he had in years of academic study. My suspicion is that the illumination he referred to was a massive expansion of his mental paradigm that allowed him to tap into the Cosmic Catalyst to a degree that few people are ever able to achieve.

Dr. Bucke's metaphysical experience never repeated itself, but he ultimately came to believe that it was the emergence of a new faculty in man that takes simple consciousness to a new level. He hypothesized that such historical figures as Jesus, Buddha, Dante, and even Walt Whitman possessed advanced consciousness on a consistent basis, while in the rest of us this genius aptitude is still evolving. In the last section of *Cosmic Consciousness*, Dr. Bucke documents numerous cases of cosmic consciousness experienced by other individuals whom he interviewed during his lifetime.

Shortly after my introduction to the work of Dr. Bucke, I read another fascinating book, *Thinking and Destiny*, by Harold W. Percival. This thousand-page tome is, to say the least, not the easiest of reading, but the author's foreword alone is worth the price of the book:

From November of 1892 I passed through astonishing and crucial experiences, following which, in the spring of 1893, there occurred the most extraordinary event of my life. I had crossed 14ᵗʰ Street at 4ᵗʰ Avenue, in New York City. Cars and people were hurrying by. While stepping up to the northeast corner curbstone, Light, greater than that of myriads of suns opened in the center of my head. In that instant or point, eternities were apprehended. There was no time. Distance and dimensions were not in evidence. . . . I was conscious of Consciousness as the Ultimate and Absolute Reality. . . . It would be futile to attempt description of the sublime grandeur and power and order and relation in poise of what I was then conscious. Twice during the next fourteen years, for a long time on each occasion, I was conscious of Consciousness. But during that time I was conscious of no more than I had been conscious of in that first moment.

As with Dr. Bucke, Harold Percival appears to have experienced a spiritual expansion of his secular belief system that brought him into sharp focus with the Cosmic Catalyst. Like Bucke, from everything I have read about Percival, his was a remarkably active life, which I do not believe to be a mere coincidence. The more action a person takes, the more expansive his mental paradigm becomes and the stronger is his connection to the infinite powers of the Cosmic Catalyst. My conviction about this is based not only on the self-evident nature of this connection, but on decades of firsthand experience.

MAGIC

When you take action—particularly bold action—the atoms in your brain vibrate at enormously high rates of speed, which often results in amazing and otherwise unexplainable "coincidences" happening in your life. I believe that the genius that erupts from action—as a result of one's connection to the Cosmic Catalyst—produces a telepathy of sorts that brings a person in contact with the people, things, and circumstances he needs to accomplish his objectives.

A person can thereby influence his results in just about any endeavor he undertakes—from getting a good grade on an exam to winning an athletic contest to making money—by taking bold action, which, in turn, stimulates his senses to find a way to bring him into contact with those elements necessary to convert his goals into physical realities.

The senses I am referring to go far beyond the obvious ones such as sight, hearing, and sensory perception. I believe that what underlies the thoughts-to-physical-realities phenomenon is that all atoms on earth—and, indeed, throughout the universe—are connected. If so, it logically follows that what happens to the atoms in your brain has an effect on atoms that are outside your body. Since atoms vibrate at tremendous speeds, whether they give off positive or negative energy is of critical importance. What determines whether the energy is positive or negative, of course, is the nature of your actions. The higher the speed of vibration and the more positive your energy, the stronger your connection to the Cosmic Catalyst.

Thinking about it in this light, distance should not be a major factor when it comes to atoms affecting one another. This, I believe, is why so many people have reportedly had telepathic experiences with family members, friends, or acquaintances thousands of miles away. On numerous occasions I have had the experience of someone calling me on the phone for the first time in many months, sometimes years, at virtually the very moment that I was thinking of him, even though I may not have had him on my mind for a very long period of time. It logically follows that the more specific the image a person holds in his mind, the more powerful and stimulating that image is when it comes to affecting other atoms.

The important thing to recognize is that, as with genius, it is action that stimulates the so-called magic to which I have been referring. And the more action you take, the more your mental paradigm waves aside the notion of the impossible, and the frequency and significance of magical events tend to increase.

POWER

Unlike genius and magic, the fact that action generates power is common science. It takes action for something to move, and when something moves, momentum is created. The stronger the action, the stronger the movement and the greater the momentum. And the greater the momentum, the more power it generates.

We see the effects of momentum in sporting events all the time. It has a habit of shifting quickly and dramatically as the actions of individuals or whole teams change. When a defensive end sacks the opposing quarterback and causes him to fumble and lose the ball, it's a violent action that produces enormous power for his team. Suddenly, the defensive team is on offense and the momentum of the entire game shifts.

What's exciting is that this is precisely how all of life works, which we would do well to remember when we get out of bed each morning. In our daily lives, however, we have much more going for us than a football team that recovers a fumble. In fact, our power is limited only by our own boldness and the amount of action we are willing to take.

In addition to action itself, the other two phenomena produced by action—genius and magic—also help to produce power. In fact, all of these factors—action, genius, and magic—build on one another to such an extent that they have the potential to create power almost exponentially.

A good technical definition of power would be "the capacity to perform effectively, to exercise control over events, and to be able to influence others." The more action we take, the more power we generate, which gives us the capacity to do great things, control events, and have tremendous influence on those around us.

For obvious reasons, inertia is at the other end of the power spectrum. Inertia is impotence personified. Using another football analogy, anyone who has ever suffered through the painful ordeal of watching his favorite team go into a "prevent defense" near the end of a game understands the impotence of inertia. Invariably, all that a prevent defense accomplishes is that it shifts the power and momentum to the other team. There are many sports fans who believe there is only one explanation for a coach switching to a prevent defense: insanity!

As is undoubtedly the case with you, I know from firsthand experience that action produces power. The story I shared with you earlier in this chapter about raising $500,000 from a German investment banker was a classic example of this. Had I listened to my attorney and not taken the initiative to call the banker, set up a meeting, and travel to New York, there's no way I would have made the deal. Trying to do it over the phone would have constituted action, but it would have lacked the boldness necessary to produce a quick *yes*.

My actions caused an expansion of my mental paradigm, elevated my resourcefulness, and motivated me to come up with alternative proposals, the very first of which the investment banker accepted. It was self-evident that the aura of power that surrounded me when I met with him in person was a result of my actually being there in the flesh. My bold action not only produced genius and magic, but also an enormous amount of power that I felt throughout our meeting.

The power I'm referring to here has nothing to do with the use of force. Nor does it have anything to do with having power over people per se (though it does give one the power to influence people). It's what I would call *pure power*—power generated from one's own well-intentioned actions. These actions work in concert with the Cosmic Catalyst only if they do not violate the natural rights of others.

THE SUCCESS CYCLE

I can say unequivocally that this is the most important chapter I've written in my career as an author. I not only believe passionately everything I have said in this chapter, but I live my own words each and every day. When there's a temporary lull in my life—when new opportunities don't seem to be finding their way to my desk—it's a signal for me to start taking action.

I see it as a success cycle: Action leads to genius and magic; action, genius, and magic work in concert to produce power; action, genius, magic, and power work together to increase motivation; and motivation leads to more action. Of course, while all this is going on, the Law of Averages sits in the background and makes time our ally so long as we continue to take action. That's because when we take action, our connection to the Cosmic Catalyst gives us a heightened state of awareness that transcends secular power and provides us with the solutions we need to solve our problems and accomplish our objectives.

I could write an entire book detailing literally hundreds of incidents in my own life where taking action produced genius, magic, and power for me, and, in conjunction with the Cosmic Catalyst and the Law of Averages, allowed me to achieve seemingly miraculous results. Words, however, can never do justice to this awesome phenomenon. It must be experienced to be fully appreciated. I highly recommend that you try it—*often*.

CHAPTER 2

Truth-Based Action

> *The truth is incontrovertible. Malice may attack it and ignorance may deride it, but in the end, there it is.*
>
> — WINSTON CHURCHILL

HUMAN BEINGS HAVE DEBATED the ultimate purpose of life throughout recorded history. If one wanted to participate in this debate, he could make a persuasive argument that the ultimate purpose of life is to search for truth. I say *search* rather than *find*, because to find truth in the broadest sense of the word would mean that one would have to know everything, and I think we can stipulate that omniscience and human beings don't match up too well.

The corollary to "nothing happens until something moves" is "something happens when something moves." When I refer to "something happens," I'm talking about a *result*. It's important to recognize that all actions produce results, regardless of their nature. But what we're after is *positive* results. And because truth is the ultimate certitude, positive results tend to flow from truth-based actions. Negative results, on the other hand, tend to flow from actions based on falsehoods or delusions.

Even if the whole world goes insane (a prospect with a reasonably high degree of probability), you have a holy responsibility to yourself to perpetually search for truth. When all about you are losing their heads, the surest way to keep yours is to be vigilant about basing your actions on truth. Truth is the foundation of rational action.

I'm not talking here about *the* search for truth or *a* search for truth. What I'm referring to is *your* search for truth. The words in this chapter—and, indeed, this entire book—represent the results of *my* search for truth. Whether you accept some, any, or all of my opinions, I will have accomplished my purpose if the results of *my* search for truth inspire you to embark upon, or intensify, *your* search for truth.

Truth is the best friend you will ever have, because, unlike people, it will never desert you in your time of need. Think of truth as a compass that points the way to actions that are in your long-term best interest. This is why your search for truth must be ongoing and in conjunction with an action-oriented life. If you ever feel as though the Cosmic Catalyst has not come through for you, it could be because your actions have not been in accordance with truth.

Unfortunately, truth is not an easy proposition. For one thing, truth can sometimes make you unpopular. In extreme cases, it has even cost people their lives. Bruno (burned at the stake as a heretic) and Socrates (forced to drink poison after being accused of corrupting youth by questioning tradition) are two well-known examples of this. As a baseline, then, anyone searching for truth must desire truth more than popularity.

As we have all witnessed, fools are often among the most popular people in society, which is a good reason not to allow your search for truth to be stifled by the widespread delusions of the masses. This is precisely why you must learn to question everything, especially so-called conventional wisdom. In the words of Buddha, "Believe nothing, no matter where you read it, or who said it, no matter if I have said it, unless it agrees with your own reason and your own common sense."

In the short term, of course, truth can be violated. A rational life, however, is based on taking actions that result in *long-term* success. Fortunately, history has repeatedly demonstrated that time is extremely kind to truth.

UNIVERSAL PRINCIPLES

All of life is based on universal principles, or laws. We cannot create or alter principles; we can only try to discover them and, once discovered, find ways to use them to our advantage. A principle is a natural law that has always existed and will continue to exist as long as there is a universe. A principle is the essence of reality.

The foundational principle of the universe, as well as all aspects of secular life, is well known to everyone: *Actions have consequences.* You cannot escape this reality, no matter how hard you try. If you delude yourself into believing otherwise and engage in negative actions, you should be prepared to bear the negative consequences of those actions.

Believing that one can create his own principles is a futile and dangerous way to live life. Of course, a person has a perfect right to go on believing whatever he wants to believe, but truth isn't discriminatory. It will hand out negative consequences just as surely to a well-meaning, ignorant individual as to one who is malicious and self-delusive. Not once has truth excused anyone for being well meaning.

Put another way, truth is Stoic in nature; it doesn't concern itself with human intentions. Truth overwhelms everything and everyone in its path. It matters not whether a violation of truth is intentional or a result of poor reasoning powers. In either case, truth yields the same consequences. Good intentions coupled with ignorance or stupidity create a tragic mix of ingredients that has a tendency to lead to bad endings. The drug that kills you has little interest in whether or not you were aware of its lethal nature.

SCIENTIFIC PRINCIPLES

Gravity is the most commonly used example of a scientific principle. We know that anything that falls within the earth's atmosphere will accelerate toward the ground at the rate of 32 ft/sec^2. There are no exceptions to this law. The same is true of molecular structure: Identical atoms under the same pressure at the same temperature will always combine to form the same molecules. Or Newton's Third Law of Motion, which states that for every action there is an equal and opposite reaction. I think it would be accurate to say that the umbrella principle for all scientific principles is: *Actions have consequences that are always in accordance with the laws of science.*

A scientific principle is truth in its purist form. When we discover scientific truths and use our creativity to apply these truths in positive ways, we accomplish positive results. Today, most of us don't give a second thought to these results, whether they be space travel, dramatically increasing food production, or producing everything from smartphones players to jumbo jets. As our understanding of scientific principles continues to accelerate, yesterday's luxuries are increasingly viewed by the average person as today's necessities. The advancement of civilization occurred at a snail's pace until about 250 years ago, when man began to dramatically accelerate his discovery of scientific principles. One way of looking at it is that man doesn't really create anything; he simply figures out new ways to rearranges atoms.

THE WAY THE WORLD WORKS

Scientific truth is not something that most of us have to consciously think about very often, but, nevertheless, we have to deal with universal principles every day of our lives. Children and politicians are notorious for either not understanding the consequences of their actions or refusing to believe that the same actions will always result in the same consequences. (It is fascinating to ponder why we punish children for not heeding the consequences of their actions, yet vote for politicians who promise to ignore history and repeat the mistakes of the past.)

On an intellectual level, most people understand the reality that truth cares nothing about whether we think it is just or unjust. Yet, they seem to continually reject this reality on an emotional level, as demonstrated by the way they live their lives. Why else would people drive while intoxicated? Or lie in an effort to get out of a tight spot? Or live beyond their means? Or commit crimes?

What makes truth such a tricky proposition is that our observations are made through the eyes of our individual conditioning. Thus, your truth may be very different from my truth because of our personal experiences, experiences that cause us to start from our own set of assumptions. For example, patriotic U.S. citizens see the flag of their country as a symbol of freedom, while many fundamentalist Islamic people see it as a symbol of oppression. The difference lies in our belief structures.

This is what happened in the infamous O. J. Simpson trial. Millions of people around the world watched in awe as they discovered, to their surprise, that a legal trial is not a search for truth. Most were appalled at how (primarily) black jurors could allow a vicious murderer to walk free. It wasn't that those jurors believed that murder was acceptable behavior. It was that their negative experiences with police blinded them to the point where they were able to ignore the overwhelming evidence and allow a band of truth-twisting attorneys to transform the proceedings into the trial of Mark Fuhrman and the Los Angeles Police Department.

What causes perceptions, and therefore conclusions, to be wrong are flawed conditioning, false premises, and false assumptions. Unfortunately, probably a majority of false premises are learned as a small child and carried through life. Since an incorrect premise or assumption is a falsehood, there is a snowballing effect; i.e., an untrue premise or assumption leads to an untrue perception, which, in turn, leads to other untrue premises, assumptions, and perceptions. All of which lead to actions that produce negative results.

In this regard, I am reminded of a story I first heard from a long-time friend, John Pugsley. Imagine you are adrift at sea. You wash up on an island, where you are taken in by a tribe of friendly, intelligent natives. You are initially thankful for your good fortune. However, you soon discover that all is not well in the village. For generations, the villagers have been engaged in a bloody, ongoing war with another tribe on the opposite side of the island. They are in a state of high anxiety over an upcoming battle, a battle that, if they win, will destroy their enemy and end the torturous war. But if they lose, it could lead to their own destruction and/or enslavement, in which case you could be a victim as well.

There is a divisive argument in progress over the strategy to be employed to win the battle. It is an argument that has raged for generations, and frequently leads to bloodshed within the tribe. The natives are in agreement with the premise that victory is possible only by appeasing the god of the volcano, but they are in dispute over how he is to be appeased.

The elder faction believes the battle can be won only if the god is appeased through the ritual murder of five of the other tribe's most beautiful maidens. The sacrifice must be carried out according to rules set down generations ago by the tribe's founders. The maidens must be captured in a raid, shorn of their hair, blindfolded with palm leaves, bound with vines, and thrown live into a boiling lake in the center of the volcano.

A second group of young radicals is convinced that the ritual has been misinterpreted. To win the battle, this group believes there should be seven maidens, not five, that they should not be shaved, and that they should be killed with a knife.

Both groups are adamant. Both are passionate. The tribe is rigidly and irreconcilably divided. In fact, subfactions are springing up that argue over the details of each plan, but all agree with the premise that ritual kidnapping and sacrifice is essential for victory; they disagree only on the details. It immediately becomes obvious to you that capturing and killing the other tribe's maidens is not the solution to the tribe's problems, but, rather, the very kind of act that has perpetuated the war.

You enter a hut and find members of the two factions studying ancient drawings of the ritual. They are arguing over a detail. The elders are uncertain only about whether the drawing means that the blindfolds should be made of palm leaves or hemp. The younger faction says that it clearly means a knife must be used. They both turn to you and insist that you cast the deciding vote. Which is the correct solution? How do *you* think the maidens should be killed?

What do you say to them? Obviously, you don't think the maidens should be killed at all, but how can you possibly make them see the gross error they are making in their search for a solution to the war? It's easy for us to see that the premise—killing the maidens—is false, but the natives on the island have been conditioned from childhood to accept this hideous premise. It has been ingrained into their belief system.

While this may sound like nothing more than a bad dream, in truth you have been cast ashore on just such an island, an island where the natives are your fellow citizens and political leaders. On a global scale, nearly 6 billion people are continuously engaged in acrimonious and bitter debate about how to solve an infinite number of problems, most of which are based on false premises.

"Peace on earth" is a noble objective, but those who believe it is possible to achieve it have not done their math very well. How do you get 6+ billion people, whose belief systems vary wildly, to agree on a moral, rational premise for peace? On the contrary, a dominant premise of a large percentage of the world's population is that most of their problems would be solved if they could just exterminate a particular ethnic or religious group. So long as people are perceived as heroes for killing members of "the tribe on the other side of the island," world peace is not possible. Plato recognized this more than 2,000 years ago when he rightly pointed out that "Only the dead have seen the end of war."

On a personal level, however, the path to success is paved with correct premises and assumptions, which, in turn, lead to correct conclusions and perceptions. Basing your actions on correct perceptions makes it infinitely more likely that you will achieve positive, long-term results.

THE ART OF TRUTH TWISTING

The search for truth as a foundation for taking positive action is made much more difficult by the fact that we are surrounded by people who spend their lives purposely trying to twist the truth to their advantage. Politicians, for example, are notoriously prolific truth twisters. While they work hard at trying to make the world believe they are acting in the best interests of their constituents, their real purpose in obfuscating the truth is to achieve their own ends.

Such lies condition our minds and lead us to false premises, which are cemented into place by those who control the education system. They do so by rewriting history, an art form that has come to be known as "revisionist history." To the extent we allow truth twisters to impact our thinking, we are less likely to take action that brings about the results *we* want and more likely to take action that gives them the results *they* want.

Through the magic of gradualism, governments have succeeded in getting people to accept a wide range of false—often absurd—premises. A classic example of this is the widely accepted notion that the president not only has the power, but the ability, to perform such miraculous tasks as "getting the economy moving" and "creating jobs."

This helps to explain why a majority of voters felt it was in their best interest to overlook Bill Clinton's lies when he was in office; things were good, and they simply did not want to rock the nation's financial boat. They truly believed that the president was responsible for America's seemingly healthy economy. It was a case of ignorance overriding morality, i.e., "Reprehensible behavior be damned, I'm not going to do anything that might kill the golden goose."

The reality, of course, is that no president can do anything to positively affect the economy other than try to get the government *out* of the economy. As for creating jobs, the only way any politician can create a job is to take a job away from someone else, either directly or indirectly. By *indirectly*, I am referring to the fact that government-created jobs take money out of the economy and thereby cause other people to become unemployed.

Government-created jobs are a result of government force, and force always interferes with the smooth workings of the marketplace. Since all government actions involve force, or, put more delicately, the threat of force, government can move the economy in only one direction: backward.

Ironically, third-world countries that are scurrying to adopt capitalism understand these realities better than do pampered Western countries. Most Americans still cling to the illusion that government not only has the moral authority to improve the economy and create jobs, but the wherewithal to do so. But they couldn't be more wrong.

An honest search for truth should reveal to any sensible adult that it is primarily entrepreneurs who create millions of jobs worldwide. In reality, entrepreneurs such as the late Steve Jobs, Microsoft's Bill Gates, and Google co-founders Sergey Bren and Larry Page have created more legitimate jobs than all U.S. presidents in history combined. In fact, if you own a hot dog stand, *you* have probably created more legitimate jobs than all U.S. presidents in history combined.

The truth of the matter is that how far man has advanced is not a reflection of his true potential; it is his true potential *minus* government interference. The premise that a president can affect the economy in a positive way is ludicrous on its face, yet, as noted, the vast majority of voters steadfastly believe it to be true. The reason for this can be found in French philosopher Michel Montaigne's observation that "Men are most apt to believe what they least understand." And since virtually no laymen understand macroeconomics (and some would argue that the same is true of professional economists), they are ripe to believe almost anything—especially if it sounds like it's going to put dollars in their pockets.

Your search for truth, then, will be flawed to the same extent that your conditioning and premises are flawed, meaning that you cannot expect to have truth on your terms. To lay down conditions in advance of searching for truth is the height of frivolity. If you want enlightenment on your terms, you will find only illusion and falsehood. A prerequisite to searching for truth as a guide to taking constructive action, then, is your willingness to let go of cherished beliefs, even if it means suffering discomfort.

THE ART OF BRAINWASHING

The spine-chilling message in the cult movie *The Manchurian Candidate* is that evil-intentioned human beings can capture the thinking mechanisms of other human beings and direct them to take actions that violate their personal moral code. The catch phrase used to describe this phenomenon is "brainwashing." Depending upon how broadly one wishes to interpret the phenomenon of brainwashing, it can include anything from mind-dulling ads on television to cult leaders who direct their followers to commit suicide.

Beer commercials, for example, seem to want us to believe that if men will just drink more beer, they can spend the remainder of their lives playing volley ball on the beach, surrounded by beautiful, bikini-clad women, and laughing hysterically. Fast-food ads appear to be telling us that if we eat more of their fat-and-salt-laden meals, we and our children will be giddy with laughter and need not be concerned with such mundane matters as heart disease, stroke, diabetes, and colon cancer. (Automobile ads are so stupid that I'm not sure what they are trying to tell us, but I must admit that a pickup truck looks rather interesting sitting alone on a mountaintop for no apparent reason.)

Interestingly, according to extensive research conducted by renowned marketing experts Al and Laura Ries, most advertising has little to do with selling products and everything to do with ad agencies' showing off their "creativity." In their groundbreaking book *The Fall of Advertising & the Rise of PR,* they document case after case of giant corporations spending millions of dollars on ad campaigns, only to have their sales go *down.*

The primary focus of ad agencies, say Al and Laura Ries, is on winning industry creativity awards. Which was a great relief to me, since I always assumed that I must be dense for not being able to figure out why anyone would buy a new automobile, a six-pack of beer, or a hamburger based on any television ad I've ever seen.

David Ogilvy, the legendary Madison Avenue advertising genius, put an exclamation point on the Rieses' research findings when he said, "The advertising business is going down the drain. It is being pulled down by the people who create it, who don't know how to sell anything, who have never sold anything in their lives . . . who despise selling, whose mission in life is to be clever show-offs and con clients into giving them money to display their originality and genius."

Which is actually very good news. It means that television commercials, because of their asinine content, are relatively harmless, and probably succeed in persuading only those with IQs of less than twenty to be lazy, ignorant, and shortsighted.

CULT BRAINWASHING, HOWEVER, CAN be quite harmful. Until I moved to New Zealand, I had never given much thought to cults other than to view an occasional Jonestown-type horror story on television. Shortly after my arrival, I developed a friendship with a highly intelligent, creative entrepreneur ("Jeremy") who possessed a fabulous work ethic. He was a persuasive, seemingly rational individual with an infectious positive attitude. I found Jeremy's insights into ideology, human relations, and health matters to be fascinating. I was convinced he had all the tools necessary not only to be successful in his own right, but to make a positive contribution to Kiwi society.

At some point in time, however, I became aware that Jeremy attended the regular weekly meetings of what he described as a "self-help group." Early on, he said to me, "I'm going to press you real hard to become involved in my self-help group," but at the time I didn't give his comment much thought.

A short while later, during one of our discussions about nutrition, Jeremy told me that his group owned an organic farm, which he invited me to visit. I accepted his invitation, and a couple of days later we made the trek a few miles out of town to the farm. At the edge of the farm was a sort of open-air shack from which group members sold homemade soups, drinks, and produce grown on site. Jeremy introduced me to two young women who were dispensing hot soup, and invited me to have a bowl.

Anatomically speaking, each of us has a microscopic alarm in our brain—referred to in higher circles of medicine as the Kosher Button—that activates when something we're hearing or seeing doesn't ring true. When I heard the two soup-serving women speak, I thought I was talking to the Stepford wives (from the movie of the same name), whereupon my Kosher Button quickly sent a message to me: *Not kosher!* I then looked carefully into their glazed eyes, and the message came back even stronger: *Definitely* not kosher!

"Your wish is our command, Oh Green One."

When Jeremy and I were walking back to our car, an elderly woman in tattered clothes said hello to him. He introduced her to me, then later explained that she was a longtime member of the group. I clearly recall thinking to myself that this woman did not appear to be the kind of person who would be involved in a self-help group to which Jeremy belonged.

In the coming weeks, I began asking various acquaintances about the group, the farm, the people I had met, and Jeremy, and was somewhat alarmed by the feedback I received. The self-help group ("Money's Gate"), it turned out, was an infamous cult that was well known throughout New Zealand. Some members, in fact, had belonged to Money's Gate for more than twenty years. I was told that Jeremy was the number-two man in the cult, just a heartbeat away from ascending the throne.

The man at the top, the cult's leader, was said to be a uniquely wise individual who preached self-responsibility. Members were taught that no excuse was justified when it came to not meeting one's commitments, which sounded like an admirable philosophy for a self-help group. Unfortunately, however, many of the group's rules and practices contradicted its purported purpose.

For one thing, every member was required to pay the leader of Money's Gate a fixed percentage of his gross weekly income. The money, I was told, was paid in twenty-dollar bills and slipped under the cult leader's back door in an unmarked envelope—or rolled up and pushed through a round hole in the same door. If the leader proclaimed the money count to be incorrect, the member did not receive credit for his contribution.

A business acquaintance told me that both of his younger brothers had been recruited into Money's Gate while still in high school. This occurred a short time after their father had died, which seemed to be a common thread in the recruitment of a number of members. (Jeremy himself had joined the cult while still in high school, a few years after his own father had passed away.) After a ten-year tenure, one of the brothers dropped out of the cult, whereupon the cult forbade the other brother to speak to him.

I also was told by several ex-members that Money's Gate had periodic feasts at which members would sit at a large table, with seating based on their status in the cult's hierarchy, and pass around sumptuous platters of food. The cult's leader would make his selections first, then pass each platter on to Jeremy. Jeremy would take what he wanted, then pass the food on to the next person in the pecking order, and so on until whatever food was left eventually found its way to the lowest member on the cult ladder.

The numerous stories that were related to me about Money's Gate could fill a book of their own, but what was perhaps most surprising was the number of people in the cult who had legitimate occupational backgrounds. Included among its members were graphic artists, cabinetmakers, accountants, and various business owners and entrepreneurs. Jeremy himself was an incredibly energetic, bright, hardworking entrepreneur who preached self-responsibility and individualism. In addition, he appeared to be both logical and rational.

All of these positive qualities notwithstanding, I ultimately became convinced that the brainwashing had gone on for far too long and that Jeremy was a "lifer."

This chilling experience made me realize that neither high intelligence nor rational action in other areas of a person's life will necessarily deter him from buying into a cult's program, notwithstanding how irrational or contradictory such a program may be. Which means that quality brainwashing has the power to triumph over quality intellect, sort of like the old baseball maxim that good pitching beats good hitting every time. This is precisely why we are surrounded by millions of intelligent people who are constantly debating how the maidens should be killed.

Rational action and brainwashing are at opposite ends of the self-determination spectrum. Rational action requires, first and foremost, that a person be in control of his mind. To the extent someone else does your thinking for you—be it television commentators, politicians, or leaders of causes—you are likely to take actions that are not in your best interest. More often than not, such actions are based on someone else's view of right and wrong, a view often camouflaged by lies.

In this regard, it is wise to heed the words of Ralph Waldo Emerson, who said, "Nothing is at last sacred but the integrity of your own mind." Anything sacred should be guarded with a passion, which is why you should never allow anyone to gain control of your greatest asset. And the best way to accomplish that is to be vigilant when it comes to relying on your own ability to think rationally as opposed to blindly accepting the opinions of others. Unfortunately, most people appear to have little motivation to think for themselves. Adolf Hitler made it clear that he was all too aware of this mental lethargy in the German populace when he cynically said, "What good fortune for government that the people do not think."

SELF-DELUSION

Many of the falsehoods we harbor are the result of self-inflicted misinformation; i.e., even though we know, or at least suspect, that the facts are contrary to our desires, we choose to ignore these facts and cling to our cherished beliefs. In psychology, the term used to describe the anxiety resulting from this self-destructive state of mind is *cognitive dissonance*. A person so afflicted simply blocks out information that contradicts his established belief structure.

In the case of my friend Jeremy, even though he had obviously experienced years of cult brainwashing, I became convinced from our discussions that adhering to his self-destructive way of life was a direct result of vigilant self-delusion. On the one hand, he preached self-responsibility and individualism, but, at the same time, he paid homage and money to the leader of Money's Gate because he believed in the cult's hierarchical structure. Clearly, his mind simultaneously held two contradictory beliefs. His anxiety and stress over this conflict were outwardly obvious to those who knew him.

LOVING TRUTH

To effectively use the search for truth as a guide to your actions, you must first come to love truth. Unfortunately, most people do not love truth; instead, they try to make true that which they love. To be committed to truth, you must be willing to subordinate your desires and wishes—your dreams, as it were—to reality.

It's okay to have dreams. However, you have to be careful not to allow your dreams to mask as reality. Your love of truth has to be more important to you than your desire to make your dreams come true.

Human disdain for truth has always been with us. More than three hundred years ago, Baltasar Gracian pointed out that "Truth is abhorred by the masses." Why do people harbor such hatred for truth? Because truth can often be harsh, and, as human beings, we quite naturally gravitate toward less pain and more pleasure. Which is fine, so long as it pertains to long-term pleasure rather than instant gratification.

We tend not to worry about what's coming down the road; we just want to feel good today. We simply do not want our self-delusive little worlds to be upset by an insignificant irritant such as truth. But the reality is that one has to be willing to experience the discomfort often associated with truth if one's objective is to take rational actions that are in harmony with one's long-term objectives.

The failure to love truth is why human beings have such a propensity for shooting messengers. Messengers are the bad guys who have an annoying habit of delivering truth. But no matter how many dead messengers we leave lying at our feet, and despite how vigorously we try to hide from truth, truth always finds a way to survive and deliver its consequences to us—and the consequences can be severe. The greater the repression of truth, and the longer the repression takes place, the graver the ultimate consequences.

The world-wide medical establishment has long been known for its vigilance in defending the status quo against maverick truth messengers. Growing up, I can remember being encouraged from all quarters (including my parents) to eat plenty of eggs, butter, milk, cheese, white bread, and, of course, lots of beef. I even vividly recall Perry Como taking a relaxing puff on his Lucky Strike cigarette on television, exhaling the fumes, then telling millions of viewers that Luckies not only tasted good, but were "good for you."

Today, of course, all this sounds like insanity, because just about everyone, both in and outside of the medical community, fully understands that these are the very things that provide the shortest route to heart disease, stroke, diabetes, and a wide variety of cancers. (*Note*: The latest medical research purportedly indicates that perhaps eggs should be taken off the axis-of-evil food list, but there is no consensus on this.)

Nevertheless, corporate giants in the dairy, beef, tobacco, and pharmaceutical industries, along with the American Medical Association, continue to take pot shots at medical messengers in an effort to repress the hated, profit-killing truth. Healthy diets and holistic medicine threaten not only the incomes of doctors, but those of hospitals, clinics, and those involved in the manufacture and sale of pharmaceuticals and surgical equipment as well. After all, if people ate only healthy food, where would the medical community get its patients?

Fortunately, nowadays the importance of a healthy, natural diet in preventing disease is pretty well accepted, thanks to "alternative medicine" professionals who have been successful in spreading the truth. In fact, today there are so many truth messengers in the medical profession that shooting them is no longer a practical solution. The rapidly increasing influence of these messengers on the general public is yet another example of history being kind to truth.

THE SOMETHING-FOR-NOTHING INSTINCT

More than any other factor, money tends to bring our something-for-nothing urge to the surface. When this happens, it's usually a case of substituting one's desires for reality. The something-for-nothing urge is programmed into the human psyche, thus, to one degree or another, we all possess it. It is this self-delusive urge, or instinct, that has made gambling a national pastime in most countries.

State governments understand the something-for-nothing instinct all too well, and they have increasingly preyed upon it to appropriate more dollars from citizens by enticing them to donate their money to state-sponsored lotteries. This is in addition to the fact that most states skim off the top from horse- and dog-track wagering, jai alai games, and casinos. With such an explicit stamp of approval, it's little wonder that more than 5 million Americans are said to be addicted to gambling.

In reality, compulsive gambling is a serious mental disorder that endangers both the compulsive gambler and those around him. It involves an extreme form of self-delusion—the belief that something for nothing is possible, which is totally against the laws of nature. What's so insidious about gambling is that a person may actually get lucky and win now and then, which only strengthens his delusion that he can win over the long term. It is this belief that constitutes a totally false perception of reality and causes him to take ever more self-destructive action.

Perhaps the most dangerous form of the gambling self-delusion is the stock market, where the dot-com collapse of the new millennium became the poster child for historic investment bubbles. No matter how many investment bubbles burst, laymen investors seem incapable of understanding that it can, and will, happen again. As management guru Peter Drucker wryly stated, "The life span of a soap bubble averages eighteen seconds. The life span of an investment bubble averages eighteen months." Given the historically long life span of the bull market of the nineties, it's no wonder that virtually everyone was seduced.

In theory, of course, investing in operating enterprises is a noble activity, because it provides liquidity to the capital markets. But the reality is that most people invest in stocks because they believe they can increase their wealth without labor. This is especially true during long bull markets, when the average investor becomes convinced that stock values will continue to rise indefinitely.

Since even the most unsophisticated stock-market participants can and do read, they certainly must know that every bull market eventually gives way to a bear market—often a nasty bear market. In addition, at one time or another, most investors have read about the many studies that have demonstrated that throwing darts at a dartboard containing the names of listed stocks often produces better results than does the careful study of many of the most highly touted stock-market experts.

"Tell us, Mr. Tortoise, how did you develop your uncanny expertise for picking stock-market winners?"

Yet, history notwithstanding, every generation insists on pushing markets beyond their breaking points, and usually those who can least afford it end up holding the badly deflated bag. There is no question in my mind that self-delusion is the culprit upon which they base their actions.

THE ULTIMATE SELF-DELUSION: IMMORTALITY

Perhaps the most dangerous self-delusion of all is the belief people seem to have in their own immortality. Of course, they don't consciously admit it, at least not to others. But in their minds, I think most people truly believe they will be the first human beings to live forever. Why else would a person smoke, take drugs, drink excessively, or eat a diet loaded with saturated fat, cholesterol, salt, sugar, and processed foods?

A wise philosopher friend of mine once asked me who the biggest mass murderer in history was. I knew it was a trick question, one to which most people give the knee-jerk response, "Adolf Hitler." The correct answer, I felt certain, was Joseph Stalin, the brutal Soviet dictator who killed more than 20 million of his own countrymen.

"Wrong," said my friend. "The greatest mass murderer in history was Ray Kroc, the founder of McDonald's." I got the message. Ruthless dictators use violence. There is no pretense of fun, no clown frolicking on television in an attempt to convince people that happiness awaits them in the gulag.

The fast-food folks, however, while publicly supporting charitable causes aimed at saving the planet and helping the poor, maintain fun-looking killing machines throughout the world—colorful little shacks filled with food weapons that turn people's bodies into medical time bombs. Prostate and colon cancer, arteriosclerosis, stroke, and diabetes, while not as spectacular as decapitations and firing squads, succeed year after year in piling up the kind of impressive fatality numbers that would make run-of-the-mill serial killers envious.

In fairness, however, don't blame the fast-food executioners if you should get killed by a deadly burger, taco, or innocent-looking piece of pizza. These guys are humble. They know full well that they couldn't do it without their customers' willingness to delude themselves.

COMING TO GRIPS WITH MORTALITY

As to cigarettes, for more than thirty years my eldest sister became angry with anyone in our family who urged her to stop smoking. In a spirit of defensiveness, she insisted that she enjoyed it, notwithstanding the fact that she was a highly intelligent, well-informed person who certainly was aware of the much-publicized facts regarding cigarette smoke.

Sadly, the day the doctor handed my sister her death warrant—a diagnosis of inoperable lung cancer—she immediately stopped smoking. She spent the rest of her days angry with herself for "being so stupid." And, of course, she didn't miss the enjoyment she once got from cigarettes. If you've ever witnessed someone close to you dying of cancer, you know that it's a pretty grim scene, one you never forget. It certainly makes you think long and hard about your own mortality.

What allows a person to engage in a dangerous activity with impunity, be it smoking, unhealthy eating, or drunk driving, is the self-delusion that he will be the one to defy the odds and escape the inevitable consequences of his actions. This view is reconfirmed every time I see another insane daredevil stunt gone wrong on television. Coming to grips with one's own mortality requires that an individual override his wishes with reality and guide his actions accordingly.

If truth is the underpinning of rational action, then the first and most critical truth to accept is the reality that you are not immortal. One's own mortality is another one of those truths that most people accept on an intellectual level, but do not really believe on a day-to-day, emotional level. That's why you must be vigilant when it comes to eliminating any self-delusions you may be harboring about your own mortality, then live life accordingly.

Ironically, the more you act on the belief that you're immortal, the sooner you are likely to find out, to your dismay, that you are not. A better idea is to live in accordance with truth and enjoy good health while you're here. The reason you must be vigilant about this matter is because you will always be surrounded by temptations to eat, drink, and partake in activities that are anti-life.

Trust me on this one: You *are* mortal. Accept this reality, be protective of your well-being, treat your body with respect, and you may just stick around long enough to enjoy a life worth living.

PERCEPTION OF REALITY

Reality is what it is. People's perception of reality, on the other hand, is a variable. By *perception*, I am referring to the ability to be able to grasp the difference between what is real and what is unreal, between actions that bring you closer to achieving your goals and actions that move you further away from those goals. A faulty perception of reality almost always leads to bad consequences and can even be fatal.

Unfortunately, most people live in a totally *unreal* world. Theirs is a world they create in their own minds based on the way they would *like* things to be rather than the way they actually *are*. In effect, they live in a state of waking dreams.

So, when people argue about whose truth is the real truth—whose perception of reality is accurate—the answer is quite simple: The individual who consistently gets positive results is the one who most often bases his actions on truth. The individual who consistently gets negative results most likely bases too many of his actions on falsehoods.

However, it's worth noting that when another person's perception of truth is inaccurate, that person's inaccurate perception becomes a reality in itself, a reality that you have to take into consideration when dealing with him. Put another way, though you may be certain that the other person's belief is untrue, his erroneous *belief*—not the facts themselves—takes on a life of its own.

Discovering truth involves courage, honesty, and a great deal of effort on your part. It must be *your* search for truth, no one else's. Above all, be conscious of the fact that, because of its finiteness, there is an urgency to life, so basing one's actions on false perceptions for even a short period of time is certain to yield bad results.

No one can go on believing whatever he wants to believe—creating his own reality—without suffering appropriate consequences. And if those consequences do not arrive until later in life, when the individual is ill prepared to handle them, so much the worse. If the prospect of middle- and old-age regret sounds painful to you, it should motivate you to start your search for truth as early as possible and embrace it whenever and wherever you find it. When it comes to truth, the future is now. There will never be a better day than today to begin your search for truth.

Despite how action-oriented you may be, it is imperative to keep in mind that if your actions are not based on truth, they are likely to produce negative results. David Seabury alluded to this in his book *The Art of Selfishness* when he said, "The comforts of self-delusion tend to be short-lived, for stubborn reality has a savage way of destroying a fool's paradise. This side of the lunatic asylum one cannot go on believing what one wants to believe. Truth will out."

As you learn to correctly perceive the world around you, delusions begin to disappear from your life. And as delusions vanish, you will find that your actions will yield correspondingly better results.

CHAPTER 3

Value-Oriented Action

Try not to become a man of success, but, rather, try to become a man of value.

— ALBERT EINSTEIN

WHETHER OR NOT YOU believe in extraterrestrial intelligence, the evidence for it certainly exists. In fact, I have long suspected that humanoids from another galaxy are walking among us, right here on planet Earth. These aliens apparently don't want to destroy us; they want only to enslave us to their benefit.

They appear to have organized a conspiracy that includes granting favors to terrestrial creatures who cooperate with them. The conspiracy revolves around a device whose purpose it is to dull our senses and steer us away from thoughts that might inspire us to take action to better our existence. The code word for this device is *xobparc* (which, by coincidence, is *crapbox* spelled backward).

English-speaking people have long referred to the crapbox device as "television set." An integral part of the aliens' conspiracy is that they have entered into deals with the Japanese (to manufacture *xobparcs*) and the television networks (to produce *eraf parc*—which, by another inexplicable coincidence, happens to be *crap fare* spelled backwards). English-speaking people refer to *eraf parc* as "television programming."

Some of the more effective *eraf parc* that the television networks have created for the aliens include such artistic offerings as:

- Shuck-and-jive ads that impart intellectual offerings such as, "The three most important words in the English language are, 'Hey, beer man!'"
- The mindless chatter that is standard fare for daytime talk shows.
- Sitcoms so asinine that they insult the intelligence of grade-school kids.
- Nonstop college and professional sporting events, seven days a week, 365 days a year.
- Wrestling, cloned infomercials, scripted reality-TV shows, and other assorted fecal offerings.

To the untold millions of people who are entrapped by this mind-dulling conspiracy, I feel compelled to offer a compassionate piece of advice: Get a life! The first step toward controlling your destiny is to escape, by any means possible, the desensitizing *eraf parc* that is available twenty-four hours a day on your dreaded *xobparc*.

More specifically, it means getting up out of your chair—*right now*—and emphatically saying, "No, I don't have to flood my brain with *eraf parc* today. I can devote my time to actions that have the potential to better my existence. I *do* have a choice."

But your *xobparc* is only one of the many mind-deadening temptations that continually beckon you. There are plotless violent movies, amusement parks, social clubs masquerading as "health clubs," and daily treks to the fast-food killing machines. None of these activities, of course, can compare to spending endless hours in front of your *xobparc* watching *eraf parc*, but all chip away at your limited time resources and prevent you from getting on with the serious and exciting business of life.

If any of this sounds at least vaguely familiar to you, it may be time for you to face the truth squarely in the eye. And the truth is that you can't expect to change your life for the better if you continue to spend inordinate amounts of time on frivolous activities. There is nothing wrong with entertainment and relaxation, so long as they don't threaten to become your full-time occupation. The fact that you are surrounded by brain-dead people is no excuse. It's up to you to have the courage and self-discipline to rise above the walking dead and start taking constructive action.

THE CURSE OF VICTIMIZATION

In the previous chapter, I pointed out that if a person's belief system is faulty, his premises also will be faulty, which, in turn, ensures false perceptions. Perhaps the best example of this is a person who is caught up in the folly of an emotional disease known as *victimization*. It's a disease that mentally paralyzes the afflicted individual, because he feels that the deck has been stacked against him. Such a misguided individual would tend to see himself as a helpless victim of an unjust world, and thus would have no incentive to take action to try to improve his life.

The disintegration of Western culture over the past half century has been the number-one culprit when it comes to encouraging people to harbor false premises that produce the phenomenon of victimization. All who embrace this self-destructive notion are doomed, at best, to mediocrity; at worst, to total failure.

If you're serious about living a meaningful life, you must, first and foremost, avoid the victimization trap. It's a trap that has been set by vote-hungry politicians, self-anointed crusade leaders, and shameless legal hucksters operating under the respectable-sounding title of "personal-injury attorney." These master truth twisters spread lies that appeal to our human frailties, negatively condition our minds, and lead us to accept false premises.

There are two major problems with victimization. First, it allows a person to harbor the poisonous belief that material gain without work is possible. Second, those who capitalize on the victimization scam do so at the expense of others. Again, if your intention is to search for truth, you must first learn to love truth. You must love truth so much that you are willing to let go of cherished beliefs. Victimization is a mind-set that makes it especially easy to confuse truth with personal desires, and desires must always be subordinated to truth.

THE MAGIC OF SEMANTICS

In order to eradicate the notion of victimization, it is helpful to back up a step and examine its roots. A human being is a creature of infinite desires, and it is quite normal to want to fulfill as many of those desires as possible. However, he is aware that merely telling people that he wants something is not likely to produce results. To overcome this problem, it has become popular to claim that whatever one desires is a "need." The transformation of a desire into a need is an integral component of victimization.

Need, of course, is a subjective word; i.e., it is but an opinion. There is no such thing as an absolute need. I may think that I need a Rolls-Royce; you may think I need a bicycle. Neither of us is right or wrong; we merely have a difference of opinion.

However, my *desire* for a Rolls-Royce is an entirely different matter. There is no opinion involved. If I desire a Rolls-Royce, that's my business. It becomes your business only if I arbitrarily decide that you have an obligation to buy it for me, on the grounds that it's a "need" and that I am therefore "entitled" to it. The fact that I may call my desire for a Rolls-Royce a *need* is, of course, semantic nonsense. I may just as well call it a *wart*, because, regardless of what word I assign to it, I still have no moral right to force you to help me acquire it just because I happen to want it.

However, this camouflage is only the first step in the semantics game that is part and parcel to victimization. The second step involves the clever elevation of "needs" to "rights." All Western cultures now accept the belief that every individual has a "right" to an education, a "right" to a "good" job, a "right" to a "minimum" wage, a "right" to "decent" housing, a "right" to virtually anything that a person can establish as "society's obligation" to him. This is quite a contrast to earlier times in America when most people believed that no one had a right to anything except life, liberty, and the pursuit of happiness.

Unfortunately, Western civilization has devolved to the point where the use of force and fraud can be easily justified on the grounds that such measures are necessary to make certain that people's "rights" are not violated, i.e., to make certain their individual *desires* are fulfilled. When all is said and done, this is what politics is all about. H. L. Mencken summed it up perfectly when he described an election as "an advanced auction of stolen goods."

There is, quite obviously, one glaring problem with the desires-to-needs-to-rights game. In order to fulfill the perceived rights of one person, another person's right to his liberty must be violated, because any product or service that an individual may desire must be produced by someone else. And if the product or service (or the money to purchase it) is taken from a productive citizen against his will, then that citizen's rights have been sacrificed to the desires of the person who receives the largesse.

The acceleration of the victimization syndrome has reached such grotesque proportions in Western society that it now accords the *victim* label to virtually everyone. Nothing deadens the soul quite like victimization. It's a trap that kills off the motivation to take action.

In this respect, perhaps the ultimate victimization trap is the insane notion of reparations for black Americans. Black "leaders" who are shamelessly promoting this cruel hoax on the black community are the only ones who will end up profiting from the mischief they create. In his eye-opening book *Scam*, Rev. Jesse Lee Peterson, who is black, bluntly summed up the reparations hoax:

> *Who will pay for reparations? I'll tell you who it will be. It will be people who don't have a racist bone in their bodies. It will be people who immigrated to this country after the Civil War. It will be people struggling to support a family. It will not be the slave owners; they're all dead. It will not be the Klansmen; most of those that are still around are so poor and backward they don't make enough money to pay the federal income taxes that will help bankroll a reparations deal.*

> *Those who will pay for the problem will be those who never had anything to do with it. . . . White Americans are not guilty of the sins of the past, and they must be careful not to fall to the anger of these socialist, destructive black leaders who want to racially divide and conquer us. Black Americans must drop their anger and realize that it is not the white American who is causing their destruction but their own so-called leaders, whose evil machinations know no end.*

Fortunately, whether you're black or white, you don't need a bushel full of artificial rights to get what you want in life. On the contrary, you can get everything you want—easier, faster, and in far greater abundance—without using government force to make others give it to you. As a bonus, when you achieve success on your own merits, it gives you a sense of accomplishment and high self-esteem. If everyone got rewarded just for being alive, self-esteem would not be possible and life would have no purpose.

IN CASE AMERICANS THINK they have a monopoly on the free-lunch game, allow me to pass along a bit of social perversity that is entrenched in New Zealand culture. In that beautiful land Down Under, a job is an asset of the employee! I know, I know—you think I'm kidding. In fact, the first time I heard this, I thought it was just a figure of speech—a way of expressing government extremism in protecting the "rights" of employees. Not so; it is a literal fact.

I found this out the hard way when I started terminating employees at a company I owned in New Zealand. That's when, to my amazement, my solicitor told me that in order to do so, I had to detail the employee's misdeeds through copious note taking over a long period of time. Further, I was required to spell out for the employee, in precise fashion, exactly what he was doing wrong. My solicitor recommended that I give the offending employee at least two letters to this effect over a period of about a month.

Worst of all, attitude—which is number one on most employers' lists when it comes to assessing the value of employees—is *not* a valid reason for termination. If an employee's only crime is that he is hateful and surly, poisoning the workplace atmosphere each day with his nasty attitude, you had better learn to live with it for as long as he chooses to work for you.

Once you cross over the line and give an employee a warning letter, it becomes a bit of a cat-and-mouse game, because the employee is well aware that you intend to terminate him. This gives him plenty of time to sabotage files, computers, and just about anything else he thinks he can get his hands on without getting caught. Of course, since you can't terminate him immediately, he also is in a position to bad-mouth you and your company to your other employees.

Then, when the other shoe is dropped (i.e., termination time), the game begins in earnest. The employee runs to a solicitor special-izing in "labor relations"; the solicitor sends a letter to the employer in which he demands, on behalf of the employee, some outrageous number of months as termination pay; then the employer responds with a much lower figure. Both parties fully understand that it's just a game, and realize that they will end up settling somewhere in the area of three-to-twelve-months' pay, depending upon the employee's tenure. (If the employee has been caught doing something illegal, such as stealing, there's a chance that the settlement could be as low as one month's severance pay. I'm not sure what the employer's financial obligation is in the case of first-degree murder.)

Sounds great for the victim-employee, right? Wrong. In reality, the job-is-an-asset-of-the-employee law is a political hoax on New Zealand employees, because it's such an outrageous law that it has evolved into a game. So employers, quite naturally, do whatever they have to do to protect themselves.

For starters, the game has approximately the same effect on employment as minimum-wage laws. Employers simply hire as few people as possible in order to reduce their risk. Second, they pay the lowest possible wages in anticipation of the day when they may have to terminate a worker, because termination pay is based on salary. So, in the end, what really happens is that an unemployed worker loses more income as a result of less hiring than would have been the case in a totally free-market economy, because on average he stays unem-ployed longer due to the job-is-an-asset-of-the-employee law. Then, when he finally does land a job, he earns a lower starting salary than he might otherwise have earned, because the employer doesn't want to set himself up for a bone-crushing termination-pay settlement in the future.

When and if the employee is terminated, all the employer does, in effect, is give him part of what he would have made in a free-market economy. I say *part*, because I am convinced that an employee would be much ahead of the game financially if the government did not interfere and take the ludicrous position that he owns his job. The moral is that government action (read, force) does not work. The results it appears to achieve are really just cruel illusions.

THE ULTIMATE WISDOM PRINCIPLE

I am reminded of a tale about a powerful king who called his wise men together and directed them to prepare a compilation of all the wisdom in the world. The wise men worked for many months, frantically researching and discussing a wide variety of subjects. Finally, they presented the king with ten volumes of information that they were confident would please him.

The king perused a few pages of one volume, then said, "This is far too much material. Surely you can give me the wisdom of the world in less than ten volumes." So the king sent his wise men back to work on summarizing the wisdom contained in their ten volumes. It took many more months, but when they were done they had reduced their findings to a single volume.

Even more confident than the first time around, the wise men handed the king their work, whereupon he again perused a few pages. Shaking his head with dissatisfaction, he looked up and said, "Still far too much. I have no intention of reading all this material. Surely the wisdom of the world can be reduced to less than a volume."

The wise men, frustrated by the king's latest request, decided to go to extremes and reduce their findings to one page. This took them only about a month, and again they were confident that the king would be pleased. To their utter amazement, however, he was not. "Still too much material," bellowed the king. "What I want is all the wisdom of the world summarized in *one sentence*." The wise men gulped. How could all the wisdom of the world possibly be reduced to a single sentence?

The good thing about this seemingly impossible task was that they knew this had to be the end of the matter. Either they succeeded in giving the king what he wanted—summarizing all the wisdom of the world in one sentence—or they had to be prepared to answer to a very angry king. The task proved to be daunting, to say the least. But, after considerable reflection and debate, they finally succeeded in condensing their findings down to a single sentence.

Proudly, they approached the throne and said to the king, "Your majesty, we have at last summarized all the wisdom of the world in one sentence," whereupon the wisest of the wise men handed the king a single sheet of parchment. The king looked at it, smiled, nodded his head approvingly, then read the sentence aloud: "There's no free lunch."

Sooner or later, we learn this truth and come to understand that there is a price for everything in life. There's a price for working hard; there's a price for not working hard enough. There's a price for saving for the future; there's a price for spending all your money now. There's a price for having children; there's a price for not having children. There's a price for having friends; there's a price for being a loner. There's a price for taking the right action, there's a price for taking the wrong action. And, yes, there's a price for taking no action at all.

What this means is that you always have to give up something in order to get something in return. The empirical evidence suggests that even though most adults understand this principle on an intellectual level, they do not accept it on an emotional level. This results in actions that a rational person would describe as *irrational*, and irrational actions are sure to produce bad consequences.

Another way to describe price paying is to view life as a never-ending series of trade-offs. Regardless of how attractive something appears to be, you should never fail to look for the negative trade-offs. This is particularly important when something looks "too good to be true," because there's no such thing as a perfect person, perfect job, perfect deal, or perfect situation.

VALUE-ORIENTED ACTION

Clearly, the wise men's summation of the wisdom of the world was 180 degrees removed from the notion of government-created rights. This is also true of any and all other schemes and attempts to gain wealth without work. The reason I have never bought a lottery ticket is that I don't want to soil my belief system with fantasies of striking it rich through pure luck. Lotteries are perhaps the ultimate free-lunch delusion, which, as previously noted, is why they are a favored method of taxation by governments throughout the world.

Sooner or later, anyone who is serious about success must be willing to discard free-lunch temptations and recognize that value-oriented action is the most certain road to the promised land. The key to getting what you want is to think value instead of rights. You have no right to someone's love, you have no right to someone's friendship, you have no right to someone's respect.

All these, and more, must be *earned*, and to the extent you create value for others, you will have them in abundance. Wealth, then, is a result of value creation, and, because it is quantifiable, it is one aspect of life that makes it very easy for you to gauge how successful your efforts have been.

The nice thing about it is that if you concentrate on value, money will follow as a natural result. There is no mystery to this truth, because underlying it is a fundamental principle of human nature. The principle I'm referring to is that human beings always attempt to do what they believe to be in their best interests.

If you can't bear to accept this fact of life, ask yourself why millions of buyers purchase foreign cars, notwithstanding the goading of people, by American auto manufacturers and autoworkers, to buy domestically produced automobiles. Not even government edicts and penalties ("tariffs") can force people to stop buying higher-quality foreign cars when given the opportunity to do so.

For decades, the same was true of the garment industry, where garment workers' unions in developed countries spent millions of dollars annually on advertising in an effort to cajole people into buying domestically produced garments instead of less expensive apparel manufactured in foreign countries. Today, however, they've pretty much accepted the fact that they simply can't compete with lower, free-market wages in Third World countries.

If you still doubt that people always attempt to act in their own best interests, try asking someone to buy your product just because you need the money. Trust me, you'll sleep much better at night if your success isn't dependent on the altruistic nature of others. Creating value for the other party is the surest way to protect yourself in a business relationship.

You can spend a fortune on legal fees and draw up a contract two feet thick, but the reality is that if you manipulate a situation in such a way that it ends up being an onerous deal for the other party, you'll only succeed in buying yourself a lawsuit. No matter what a contract says, no one will continue to put effort into a venture if it becomes obvious that there is no benefit to him, especially if the other party is profiting from it.

Where the marketplace is concerned, the reality is that consumers have no interest in a company's needs, costs, or problems. What they are interested in is what the company's products or services can do to make their lives more pleasurable or less painful, which is why it's so important to understand the truth about self-interest. It is a human instinct that operates independently of our consciousness, so protestations to the contrary are irrelevant.

The late B. F. Skinner, collectivist psychologist and social theorist, spent his life searching for a scientific way to repress the human instinct to better one's existence. Skinner, by focusing on the modification of human behavior, was inadvertently acknowledging that self-interest is a natural and normal human characteristic. Only force can prevent human beings from acting in their own best interests.

Two excellent corporate examples of what happens when customer loyalty collides with customer self-interest are Wang and Xerox, both of whom were early leaders in the computer field. They didn't produce computers, per se, but, rather, dedicated word processors. Xerox produced a tank-sized machine called the Xerox 860, with an operating system that had to be reloaded each morning. Wang's machines looked much more like today's modern computers, and were far quieter than the Xerox 860. For many years, it seemed as though every office you visited had either Xerox or Wang word processors, and the two companies appeared to be way out front in the computer market.

However, led by Apple, the rest of the industry was moving toward multitask computers, and word processing was just one feature of these much more sophisticated machines. Xerox, whose arrogance is legendary in the world of big business, ignored the army of hi-tech whiz kids coming on the scene, feeling confident that its customers would remain loyal. Naively, it didn't understand the principle of self-interest. When Xerox finally woke up, it was too late. I got rid of my last Xerox 860 in the mid-1980s, years after it had been taking up too much space in my garage. Because its value had fallen to zero, I had to pay someone to haul it away.

With Wang, it appeared to be more a matter of ignorance than arrogance—though the two seem to go hand in hand—and the result was worse than that of Xerox. After years of floundering, the company finally ousted the founder's son from his CEO position and ultimately filed for bankruptcy. Wang later tried to revive itself in selected countries, but it was far too late. When it finally peeked out of its time capsule, it gazed at a brave new world dominated by strange names like Microsoft, Compaq, and Apple.

The fact that people are programmed to act in their own best interests is *why* you have to bring value to the marketplace. Giving others what *they* want motivates them to give you what *you* want. And a tough marketplace it is. In today's world of unlimited marketplace choices, the attitude of consumers is: "So what? What's the big deal? Why should I buy your product?" They are overwhelmed with offers and products, and, as a result, have become incredibly jaded.

Keeping this in mind, if you're involved in selling a product—and virtually everyone is, even if the product is himself—you had better convince people in a hurry when it comes to selling them on the merits of that product. An old marketing axiom says:

Tell me quick,
And tell me true;
Otherwise sir,
To hell with you.

Clearly, if you want to sell someone on yourself or your product, you have to get to the point quickly. Tell the prospect everything that you or it can do for him, and don't waste his time with hyperbole. *Better, faster,* and *cheaper* are three magical words to remember when thinking about how to create value.

It's also crucial to recognize that you can't sell people what you think they *should* want; consumers buy only what they *do* want. Likewise, an asking price is nothing more than your opinion of what your product or service is worth; value is someone *else's* opinion of what your product or service is worth. And, guess what? Customers aren't interested in your opinion. Which means that the virtue of self-interest in the marketplace is that no one can continue to produce a product if there aren't enough people who want to buy that product at the price that is being asked for it.

In simple terms, then, a big part of getting what you want in life is a result of taking actions that give other people what *they* want. And the one thing they want above all is good customer service and a good attitude from a company's employees.

Success becomes an almost easy proposition when you practice three simple rules:

1. If you want more, make yourself worth more.
2. Concentrate on quality and service first, and profit will follow almost automatically.
3. Always give people more than you expect to get in return.

CUSTOMER-SERVICE RULES

My father was the most customer-oriented businessman I've ever known. He had two firm rules when it came to the treatment of customers. First, when a customer comes in, stop whatever you're doing and give him *all* of your attention. Second, never argue with a customer, no matter how wrong you may believe him to be.

Which brings us to today's world of laziness, incompetence, negligence, and sloth. Since so few employees in today's minimum-wage, chain-store world have the slightest interest in pleasing customers, the individual who displays a customer-oriented attitude stands out like a professional basketball player without tattoos. The attitude of an employee toward both his employer and his employer's customers should be, "How may I be of the greatest service to you?" Every time you run into rudeness, poor service, or indifference toward customers, you're witnessing a business that is actively inviting competition.

DEALING WITH MS. TWITHEAD

As a perfect example of what *not* to do, if you'd like to go into the deli business, I can almost guarantee you success within a mile of where I used to live. There was a deli near my home that had pretty good food, and my wife and I frequented it several times a week for about a year. We usually picked up sandwiches to go, and because we saw the owner so often, we developed an amiable relationship with him.

One day we came in to order some sandwiches to bring home, and I noted that it was a new girl ("Ms. Twithead"), perhaps eighteen years of age, taking our order. Not having much confidence in either deli order-takers or eighteen-year-old kids, I made certain to emphasize to her that the order was "to go"—repeating those exact two words perhaps four or five times.

When she finally finished preparing our order, she handed it to us—you guessed it—*unwrapped and on paper plates*. I reminded her, in a pleasant tone, "Uh, I said the order was to go." To which she quickly snapped at me, "No, you didn't." Just then the owner happened to walk by, and I told him that I would appreciate it if he would tell Ms. Twithead to try to keep her lips tightly sealed and pack up our order, whereupon she again lashed out, "He *didn't* tell me the order was to go."

By now, of course, I was wondering how I could have managed to get myself into such a ridiculous situation, so to put the matter to rest once and for all, I said to the owner, in a calm, friendly voice, "It's okay, no problem. Just have her wrap the order to go. But you really should explain to this young lady the basic business philosophy that the customer is always right."

This undoubtedly would have been the end of the matter, but I had forgotten that the deli owner was originally from New York.

With a thundering fury, he responded, "The customer is *not* always right! The customer is *not* always right! I can always find plenty of customers, but I can't find decent employees." As you can well imagine, Ms. Twithead, having had her muddled, eighteen-year-old view of the world vindicated, immediately flashed an ear-to-ear grin. Whereupon a fascinating question rumbled through my mind: If this deli-dummy owner talks this way to his *best* customers, how does he treat his *worst* customers? Does he throw spoiled liverwurst at them?

As you might have guessed, neither I nor my wife ever returned to his deli. In addition, later that day I happened to mention what had transpired to a friend of mine, who also was a longtime customer of the deli, to which he replied, "Thanks for telling me; I'll never go back there again, either. I can't stand that kind of attitude toward customers."

Another question: How many other customers do you think the deli owner has lost as a result of his "the customer is not always right" attitude? Why in the world would a business owner take such a self-destructive attitude toward people who pay his rent? Who knows? Maybe he's insane; or just plain stupid; or simply mad at the world. Whatever his reason, the customer doesn't care; customers are totally self-centered. They want to know only what *you* can do for *them*—better, faster, and/or cheaper. If your life's purpose is to enhance the self-esteem of eighteen-year-old teenyboppers, best you stay out of the business world and open a prep school specializing in Disrespect 401.

WHEN THE PRODUCT IS YOU

If an employee isn't interested in creating value for his employer's customers, the least he should be interested in is increasing his own worth to his employer. In this regard, always think of yourself as a product, and recognize that a product with an enthusiastic, cooperative attitude has great value in the marketplace; a product that turns out quality work has great value in the marketplace; a product that completes projects quickly has great value in the marketplace; and a product that can solve problems has an *enormous* value in the marketplace.

In fact, the surest way to get a promotion and pay raise is to be a problem solver. All employers need problem solvers, because all employers have problems. The greater the employer's problems, the greater the opportunities for problem solvers. It goes without saying that inertia doesn't solve problems; *all problem solvers are action oriented.* There are no exceptions to this rule.

WHEN I FIRST MOVED to New Zealand, I inherited an office staff of thirteen after buying the New Zealand and Australian licensing rights to a line of health products. There's a lot of adjustment to living in a foreign country, so things were somewhat difficult in the early going. I couldn't seem to get anything done. I needed everything from paper clips to a new computer, I needed to get my files organized, I needed to put new policies and procedures into place. The list was endless.

Everyone in the office seemed to be working hard in his area of expertise, so I didn't want to take anyone away from his job to help me. However, there was a middle-aged woman ("Mary") who seemed to be functioning as a de facto office manager, and who looked as though she was knowledgeable about everything that was going on in the office. I noted that Mary's dress code was very professional and that she displayed a considerable amount of Kiwi confidence. However, I also noted that she had a foreboding aura about her, seeming always to display an unpleasant expression.

Notwithstanding her perpetual frown, I felt that Mary might be a good bet to become my executive assistant. Before making such an offer, however, I thought it would be wise to delegate some tasks to her and observe her performance. It wasn't just her skills I wanted to know about. I also wanted to observe her attitude, as I have always placed a very high premium on attitude when it comes to assessing value.

To get things started, I buzzed Mary one day and asked her to come into my office. However, to my surprise, she said that she was "busy with some other important matters." She told me that she would stop by my office when she was able to "break free." Several hours later, Mary finally came to my office and asked me what I had wanted. I told her that I would like to see how she handled some projects that I needed done, but I purposely did not tell her that I was thinking about the possibility of her becoming my executive assistant. I was prepared to offer her a substantial pay raise if she demonstrated that she was the right person for the job, but I didn't want that fact to skew her performance.

Mary's response nearly took my breath away. Increasing the intensity of her perpetual scowl, she informed me that she already was overloaded with work and therefore would not be able to help me at that particular time. Nice, Mary . . . very nice. Dumbfounded, I recalled some words of wisdom once passed along by Jerry Jones, owner of the Dallas Cowboys, in a television interview about his firing of Dallas' head coach, Jimmy Johnson.

Said Jones, "If I have to remind an employee that I'm the boss, I've been doing something wrong." With this bit of inspiration lodged in my reptilian brain, the next day I was determined to be firm with Mary. I decided to go to *her* office and tell her that I wanted to see her immediately. I was getting further behind in my work by the minute, and becoming ever more desperate for help. Notwithstanding Mary's self-destructive attitude, I made up my mind that I was going to make it easy for her to turn things around—for both her sake and mine.

However, as I began to walk out of my office, Mary happened to be rushing past my door. Instinctively, I raised my hand, right index finger pointed upward, and said, in a pleasant, almost deferential tone, "Oh, Mary, could I see you for a moment in my office?" She never even looked back, choosing instead to continue walking briskly to her demise. Waving a hand over her shoulder in a brush-aside manner, she retorted, "I can't talk now. I'm very busy." Sure, Mary.

At this point, considering the somewhat aggressive visions running through my mind, I found myself thinking how lucky I was that New Zealand had outlawed capital punishment. I was concerned that if much more time passed without my taking firm action, Mary might end up asking me if I would like to become *her* assistant. Antiquated homicide laws aside, now I was *really* getting desperate to find someone to help me. Convinced that no one else in the office was right for the job, I was

on the verge of giving up and submitting to the masochistic ordeal of working with an employment agency to fill my needs.

Then, figuratively speaking, a funny thing happened on the way to the employment agency. As I passed through the reception room on the way to my office the next morning, I said hello to the receptionist, a young lady who was generally looked upon by the rest of the office staff as an airhead. What struck me on that particular morning was her smile—a wide, toothy grin that spoke worlds to me.

I couldn't help but note the contrast between her smile and Mary's trademark frown.

Impulsively, I asked, "Joanne, how would you like to do a couple of projects for me this morning?" To which she immediately responded, "I'd *love* to, Mr. Ringer." I had her follow me to my office, then handed her a stack of newspaper tear sheets containing an advertisement that our company had just run. "I'd like you to fold each of these tear sheets neatly into quarters, put them in a pile with all of them facing in the same direction, then bring them back to me as soon as possible," I instructed.

I had given out many test projects such as this throughout my career, the object being to (1) observe the individual's attitude with regard to my asking for both neatness and speed, (2) see how quickly she completed the project, and (3) determine how literally she interpreted the word *neatly*. In Joanne's case, she immediately and enthusiastically responded, "No problem. I'll take care of it right away." In much less time than I anticipated, she returned to my office and proudly placed the tear sheets on my desk. They were folded and stacked in a perfect pile precisely as I had requested. The next thing out of her mouth was, "Is there anything else I can do for you, Mr. Ringer?"

As you might have guessed, I hired her on the spot as my executive assistant. Happily, her attitude and skills turned out to be far better than I ever could have imagined. Joanne, the twenty-one-year-old airhead receptionist whom no one in the office had taken seriously, proved to be one of the most competent people who ever worked for me. Skills and training? They didn't matter, because she was so bright and enthusiastic—so teachable—that she picked up on everything incredibly fast. Throw in loyalty beyond the call of duty, and I guess you'd have to call her the draft pick of the century.

Watching Joanne grow over the years has been a source of great delight for me. Today, she is mature and highly skilled, and as enthusiastic as she was during her first encounter with me. But when she initially became my assistant, the office staff didn't know what to make of her. Image is a fascinating thing. Imagine one day having a perception of an individual as an airhead receptionist, and the next day seeing her as assistant to the executive chairman.

Luckily, notwithstanding the staff's misperceptions of her, Joanne was ready to assume major responsibility from the outset. Within a matter of months, she took full control of the office and got things into the exact shape I wanted. Her forte, of course, was problem solving. While others moaned on endlessly about why something couldn't be done, or how difficult it was to do, Joanne was busy doing it.

As for Mary . . . well, she wasn't exactly thrilled with how things turned out. I was told that for some time she kept a Joanne doll in her home, but had eventually dismembered it and tossed the body parts into her fireplace.

Many months later, when I finally set in motion Mary's inevitable termination, she said to me—her finest scowl perfectly in place—"I know you've never liked me and that you've been trying to get rid of me from the very beginning." My initial impulse was to tell her that, on the contrary, what I really had been hoping to do from the outset was make her my executive assistant and give her a substantial pay raise, but that she hadn't been able to find the time to discuss the matter with me. I even thought about trying to explain to her that it would be much to her advantage if she worked on changing her unpleasant attitude and concentrated on ways to create value for whomever her next employer might be.

Instead, I mumbled a few meaningless, gratuitous words, wished her luck, and told her to have her solicitor call me so we could begin playing the settlement game. The reason I didn't tell Mary what I was really thinking was that I knew her well enough by then to be convinced that the truth was the last thing in the world she would want to hear. It didn't take a master's degree in psychology to be pretty certain that Mary had experienced problems with every job she had had, and that she was a person with a desperate need to blame others in order to avoid the unthinkable task of searching for the truth in her own mirror. I wondered how many other employers in her past had heard her accuse them of not liking her and wanting to get rid of her. Worst of all for Mary, how many *future* employers would hear the same kind of victimization talk coming from her lips?

Had Joanne been as cavalier in response to my requests as Mary was, I might have hired another assistant through an employment agency, which would have caused Joanne's potential value to me to decrease dramatically. And to the extent the new assistant created value, Joanne's value, in turn, would have dropped even more. This is just one of many experiences that have taught me that time is of the essence when it comes to creating value.

In simple terms, Joanne created value by swiftly taking action and solving problems; Mary, because of her atrocious attitude, *was* a problem. Watching Joanne in action reminded me all over again that attitude is to value creation as water is to a garden, because value tends to grow in direct proportion to attitude. The exalted position I offered Joanne had nothing whatsoever to do with her skills, because she possessed very few marketable skills at the time. But it had everything to do with her willingness to do whatever was asked of her—*right now*.

THE POWER OF PASSION

In Chapter 1, I pointed out that if you force yourself to take action, motivation will follow. Your creative juices will start to flow, and you will become increasingly motivated to keep right on taking action. But to the extent your motivational fires are stoked by passion, your actions will increase in both frequency and intensity. The ideal, then, is to become *passionately* motivated.

How do you develop passion? If you came home one day and found your house in flames and your family trapped inside, you would probably develop an instant passion so strong that you would try to make your way through the flames in an effort to save your family. What would cause such an instant passion is *purpose*. Your purpose would be immediately clear. It also would be clear to you that time was a limiting factor, thus you would spring into action without feeling the necessity to enter into a prolonged discussion with anyone about the matter.

If I saw you working with that kind of passion in a business setting, I'd probably offer you just about anything to persuade you to join my team. Of course, it's unlikely that you could ever be as passionate about business as you would be when trying to save the lives of your family, but it's certainly a good goal to shoot for. The closer you can come to duplicating that kind of passion in other aspects of your life, the more likely you are to create value.

The challenge, then, is to find a way to bring about passion in your day-to-day life, i.e., without the need for something as extreme as a family emergency to motivate you. I've given this challenge a lot of thought over the years, and I believe the solution lies in developing a meaningful purpose to life. Finding a meaningful purpose leads to passion, and, as noted, passion, in turn, increases the frequency and intensity of one's actions.

I like to think of this phenomenon as "passionate anticipation," a passion for what one believes the future holds. Alexander Graham Bell, with somewhat stronger credentials than I, shared his thoughts on this subject when he said, "What this power is I cannot say; all I know is that it exists and it becomes available only when a man is in that state of mind in which he knows exactly what he wants and is fully determined not to quit until he finds it."

I cannot emphasize enough that *action is the first cause*, the ignition key that starts your motivation motor running. Don't make the mistake of taking years to figure out your mission in life. Take action *now*, and gear it *toward* finding your mission in life. The genius, magic, power, and motivation generated by action will guide you to your purpose, and the more you zero in on a meaningful purpose, the more passionate you will become.

Paraphrasing Robert DeRopp from *The Master Game*, make it a point to seek a game worth playing. Having found the game, play it with intensity. Play as if your life and sanity depend upon it, because they do. The right game makes life worth living, so the challenge is to find *your* game—a game worth playing, a game you enjoy. And from a financial standpoint, make sure it's a game that creates value in the marketplace. Take action today—*continuous action*—and a value-creation game worth playing will make its appearance. As Winston Churchill put it, "Continuous effort, not strength or intelligence, is the key to unlocking our potential."

Finally, never forget that the one absolutely certain thing about life is that circumstances continually change. As a result, with the passage of time, our priorities shift, often without our being consciously aware of it. Because of this, you should periodically step back and review your progress, and if you don't seem to be getting to where you want to be in life, it's no cause for alarm. Just reevaluate the actions you've taken to date, and make any necessary course corrections. The important thing is to not become sedentary, either mentally or physically. No matter how much the world around you changes or what mistakes you make, keep right on moving—*because nothing happens until something moves.*

CHAPTER 4

Virtue-Based Action

*There are nine hundred and ninety-nine patrons
of virtue to one virtuous man.*
— HENRY DAVID THOREAU

Achievement in business, love, friendship, or any other area of life
does not precede personal growth; it follows it. It's very important not
to attempt to reverse the order of this principle. What I'm referring to
is "personal infrastructure," the virtues that make you who and what
you are. The sum total of your virtues is what gives character to your
soul. A weak personal infrastructure is the foundation for actions that
lead to negative results. A strong personal infrastructure is the foundation for actions that lead to positive results.

There are two issues involved here. The first is how others perceive
you (and remember you after you're gone); the second is what you
really are inside. How others perceive you may affect the quality of
your daily life, but it cannot affect the character of your soul.

However, the foundation of every civilization is a generally
accepted code of conduct, or standard of behavior, and within the
framework of the civilization of which you are a part, the reality is

that you are judged by others. Further, it's human nature to want others to perceive you in a positive light. You are judged first by how you look; second, by what you say; third, and most important, by your actions.

What you do to embellish your physical appearance—from wardrobe to hairstyle—has both a short- and long-term impact on how others perceive you. But your *natural* physical appearance—i.e., wardrobe and hairstyle aside—has only a very short-term impact on the perception of those who meet you. Think of the ten people whom you most admire. Is your admiration for any of these people based on their physical attractiveness? Hopefully not. Most likely, you admire them for their accomplishments and/or character.

Fortunately, we all pretty much agree on which traits are virtuous. We agree because, modern-day relativism aside, certain things "feel right" and certain things "feel wrong." Basing your actions on the fundamental virtues of Western culture is a smart strategy if your goal is to lead a happy and prosperous life. It would take a very big book to cover all the virtues that are important to most of us, which include such things as compassion, flexibility, forgiveness, hard work, kindness, patience, persistence, respectfulness, temperance, and tolerance.

For purposes of this book, however—emphasizing the importance of virtue-based actions as a key ingredient for achieving positive, long-term results—I have selected seven virtues that I believe to be of special importance. But I want to emphasize that in no way are my selections intended to diminish the importance of any of the other commonly admired virtues of Western culture. In truth, they are *all* important.

CIVILITY

Recently, I felt like doing something outrageous, so I stopped at an ice cream shop in a nearby strip mall. Inside was a familiar scene: rock music blasting in the background, a young man with long, unkempt blond hair behind the counter, and a group of pals hanging around and gabbing with him. After I waited a couple of minutes for the young man to begrudgingly excuse himself from his social obligations, he turned to me and snarled, "Yeah?" (His version of, "May I help you, sir?")

"I'd like a chocolate chip cone, please," I said. Without so much as a grunt, he inserted two dirty fingers inside a cone and carried it over to the ice cream containers. With his unwieldy hair dangling into the chocolate chip ice cream, he then proceeded to mash a dip of ice cream onto the cone, wipe his nose with the back of his right hand while handing me my ice cream cone with his left hand, and mumble, "Here ya go." (His version of, "Here's your ice cream cone, sir.") Trying hard not to show my nausea, I paid for the cone, walked outside, and tossed it into the first trash container I spotted. So much for doing something outrageous.

I then got in my car and started driving home when, about block from the mall, I saw through my rearview mirror a pickup truck bearing down on me. Not just any old pickup truck, but one of those silly-looking getups where the body sits atop tires that look like they were made for a 747 aircraft. As the driver began pounding away on his horn in an attempt to intimidate me into pressing harder on the gas pedal and exceeding the speed limit, I tapped my brake a couple of times to keep him from rear-ending me. The punk kid behind the wheel almost went berserk. He put the truck into overdrive and came roaring up beside me. Road rage! With his ball cap dutifully worn in the "up yours" backward position, and iridescent-rim sunglasses firmly in place, he shouted a remarkable array of obscenities and flipped me the obligatory bird.

Finally, I arrived home. Now I could relax and lock out the insanities of the modern world. I turned on the television set, only to be greeted by some rude, foul-mouthed weirdos who were expounding on their "rap philosophy" for an interviewer. Employing my weapon of last resort—the remote control—I quickly zapped the rappers.

The evening news would be safe, I thought to myself. A reporter was talking to a guy in his early twenties adjacent to his car. The reporter, noting that the young man's car radio had been loudly blasting rock music at an intersection, wanted to know what he thought of a proposed law that would make it illegal to play a car radio loud enough to be heard beyond ten feet. His answer was stimulating: "Ah figure it's mah right to play mah radio as loud as ah please, and if the guy next to me don' like it, he kin jus' roll up his winda and hang a hard right." Peace-loving soul that I am, thoughts of the death penalty for car-radio blasting flashed through my mind.

Two Tylenols later, I again changed channels. Aha! Just what I needed—*The Jerry Springer Show*. That day's topic was married couples with gay lovers. What more could I ask for? With thoughts of capital punishment again dancing through my head, I called up a philosopher friend of mine, hoping to get some reassurance that I was overreacting. Thankfully, he pontificated on how the world is always in the process of changing, and that what appears to be offensive today will probably be considered mild by tomorrow's standards. Whew! What a relief. And here I thought Western civilization was in trouble.

Satisfied that all was well, I leaned back in my easy chair and reflected on how lucky Americans are. A person can relax in his home without worry, knowing that there are whole armies of people out there to protect him. The ACLU fights for our right to say and do anything that happens to suit our fancy and prevents the authorities from "profiling" people who strongly resemble known terrorists. Politicians protect us from partaking in victimless crimes. And, thankfully, we don't need to worry about dangerous people taking advantage of us, because we have federal prosecutors to put (or try to put) uncivilized monsters like Michael Milken and Martha Stewart in jail.

I felt such a sense of security that I even thought about going back to the ice cream shop and trying for another chocolate chip cone. I decided against it, however, when I began picturing strands of dirty blond hair stuck in my intestinal tract. Besides, being the considerate person I am, I didn't want to be responsible for once again interrupting the teen-babble session that the kid behind the counter was having with his pals.

PEOPLE OFTEN GET DISCOURAGED by the moral decline of Western civilization, and there's certainly good reason for such discouragement—young people who rarely give up their seats to adults on a bus or subway; bare-chested, drunk, obnoxious fans who have taken over most sports stadiums; and movies that offer foul language, explicit sex, and stomach-turning violence, to name but a few examples.

The good news, however, is that you can choose not to succumb to the madness of the crowd. You can't do a great deal to stop the decadence that surrounds you or to change the morality of society as a whole, but that doesn't mean you have to contribute to it. You are the only person on earth who can totally control the character of *your* soul. In today's world of rudeness and impudence, actions based on civility may seem like anachronisms, but they command the admiration and respect of those who matter most—other civilized people. There's nothing that breeds bad human relations as easily and quickly as uncouth, rude, or vulgar behavior.

DIGNITY

Dignity is not a finite subject, because there are endless ways in which a person can lose his dignity—e.g., chasing after people who do not show him respect, kowtowing to the wealthy and powerful, or just acting childish.

As my first book rose to the top of the bestseller lists, I was invited to appear on most of the major talk shows. *The Tonight Show* was considered to be the pinnacle for authors, so when I was afforded the opportunity to be a guest on the show, I was quite excited. A ten-minute stint on *The Tonight Show* could sell thousands of books.

This was early in my career, and I was not aware that talk-show producers are primarily interested in guests who possess in their arsenals something that is commonly referred to in show business as a *shtick*. A shtick can be almost anything that makes a guest stand out from the norm, the more outrageous the better.

Today, the shtick of choice is sexual deviation of one kind or another, although convicted felons are also near the top of the list of welcome guests. At that time, however, just having written a book with a shocking title like *Winning through Intimidation* was good enough for me to qualify. On meeting the talent coordinator, he warned me that the producer didn't like boring guests, and that I should "play up the intimidation thing real big." Though I felt uneasy about his instructions, I mentally waved aside my concerns. Instead, like the obedient little tortoise I was, I assured him it would be no problem.

However, when the night of my scheduled appearance finally arrived, the same feeling came over me. While waiting to be called as a guest, I felt as though something wasn't right, but before I could get too deeply into my thoughts, I was told it was my turn to go on stage. I was whisked away by a bearded young chap in faded blue jeans, led through a maze of bland corridors, and told to stand behind the stage curtain until I heard my name announced.

As soon as the guest host, McLean Stevenson, bellowed my name, I came bouncing out from behind the curtain in my best

Hollywood stride and made my way to the guest chair. Right off the bat, Stevenson asked, "So tell me, how do you intimidate people?" I smiled outwardly, but inside I winced, because my book was not about how to be an intimidator. On the contrary, it was about how to *defend* oneself *against* intimidating people, which was 180 degrees removed from the question Stevenson had posed.

Repressing my discomfort, I put on my best shtick face and said, "Well, for example, the fact that you're sitting behind that desk on a raised platform is very intimidating to a guest." Whereupon

"Okay, babe, now it's your show. Let's see some intimidation."

Stevenson, as I had calculated he would do, got up out of his chair and retorted, "Heck, if that's a problem, *you* sit behind the desk and I'll be *your* guest." The crowd roared its approval as though it were about to witness a mud-wrestling event between two midget transvestites. I could feel my shtick gears turning faster and faster inside my brain. Play my cards right, and, who knows, I could become another Richard Simmons.

I jumped up from my chair, stepped onto the raised platform, and seated myself behind the host's desk. With the audience still howling with laughter, Stevenson challenged me, "Okay, babe, now it's *your* show. Let's see some intimidation."

Hard as it is to believe today, I smoked an occasional cigar during that period of my life, and I happened to have one in my breast pocket. Realizing that I needed to quickly come up with an attention-getting piece of shtick in order to reinforce the image that the producer and Stevenson wanted me to project, I whipped the cigar out of my pocket, slowly and with great drama peeled off the cellophane wrapper, stuck the cigar in my mouth, and lit it up with a flame-thrower-size burst shooting from my cigarette lighter.

I thought the audience's reaction couldn't get any more raucous, but when I proceeded to blow a smoke ring in Stevenson's direction, pandemonium broke out. Thoughts of running for president (of the National Association of Clowns, Bozos, and Criminal Defense Attorneys) shot through my mind. Could it get any better than this? With good enough shtick, anything might be possible!

Being high on shtick is like no other drug, because it doesn't abuse your body in any way. What it does, however, is abuse your self-esteem. Shtick is at the far (i.e., wrong) end of the Dignity Spectrum. After the show, as I started to awaken from my trance, sanity began to grip me. An annoying little voice from deep within my brain admonished, "You, sir, have just made an ass of yourself in front of 10 million people."

In the days that followed, I had a severe shtick hangover. I couldn't look in the mirror. My actions were not only undignified, they were misleading. On national television, I had encouraged an audience of millions of people to believe that my book was about how to become a master intimidator, which it most definitely was not. I had compromised my integrity by playing the role the big boys had expected of me.

The short-term exhilaration quickly turned to humiliation. Long term, however, it was one of the best things that ever happened to me, because it was such a degrading experience that I never forgot it. My vigilance when it comes to acting in a dignified manner remains to this day, and I am especially wary of people who want me to present an artificial persona in order to further their personal agendas.

THE EMBARRASSING LITTLE TALE above underscores how easy it is to inadvertently compromise one's dignity. Dignified action leads to self-respect, which, in turn, gives you the confidence to take more action. Unfortunately, dignity is a rare commodity in our bizarre modern-day world. We see confirmation of this all around us in such phenomena as:

- Talk shows that feature tragic people who emotionally and psychologically disrobe themselves in public while sharing their most intimate thoughts with millions of strangers.

- Attorneys who routinely advertise on radio, television, and even billboards, urging prospects to demand their rights through legal action, though not that many years ago such tacky solicitations would have resulted in an attorney's being disbarred.

- A tidal wave of verbal sloth. The "F word" has long been the *in word*, especially among teenagers. Worse, news commentators on the major networks routinely use incorrect words and phrases such as "*very* unique" (unique means "one of a kind"), "*ir*regardless" (no such word), and "he is a man *that* always finishes first" (*who* always finishes first). And, of course, the word *like* is inserted in front of virtually every sentence, as in, "Like . . . I mean . . . what's a Valley Girl (or Caroline Kennedy) supposed to do?"

- Doctors and other professionals who wear casual clothes, even blue jeans, to the office.

- Role-model, multimillionaire athletes who fill mind-dulling interviews with meaningless, trite comments such as, "That's what it's all about."

- Millions of people worldwide who surrender their individuality and throw in their lots with political-action groups who demand their "rights" (i.e., insist that government fulfill their desires at the expense of others).

- Decadent halftime entertainment at major sporting events. Janet Jackson's bare breast is probably more memorable than the game itself in the 2004 Super Bowl.

I should point out that there is a fundamental misconception about dignity in our age of expanded "rights." Political-action groups love to babble about being treated with dignity, as though dignity were a right. But dignity is no more a right than love or friendship. The reality is that no one can be forced to treat you with dignity. Through a variety of applied pressures, someone might feel that it's in his best interest to *pretend* to treat you with dignity, but such false dignity breeds only hatred and resentment. So-called political correctness is a perfect example of this, so much so that it has evolved from resentment to comedy. When a concept is no longer taken seriously, where's the dignity?

Sadly, America is now in the throes of a politically correct intellectual dark ages. Political correctness advocates now claim that more than 1 million college students have been victims of "ethnic violence"—which includes insults! (Upon hearing this, I immediately called my attorney and demanded that he file lawsuits against 7,248 people who have insulted me—in the last year, that is.) Some call it *political correctness*; I call it *insanity*.

If violence now includes insults—insults that are defined by campus radicals of the 1960s who now control the centers of higher education in most Western countries—then all my dictionaries are outdated. Violence is the use of physical force with an intent to do harm. Insults are a part of free speech, and subject to individual interpretation, at that. The road to a society where racism is minimal is paved not with coercion, but self-respect, and it is self-respect that leads to dignity. Self-respect, as noted earlier, stems from personal virtuosity; thus, dignity is derived from *within*. And from self-respect flows the respect of others—*as a natural consequence.*

In other words, civility has to do with how you treat *others*; dignity has to do with how you treat *yourself.* You do not have a right to be treated with dignity. You do, however, have a right to *possess* dignity. Demanding dignity from others is the ultimate self-delusion. If being treated with dignity is really important to you, the best way to bring that about is to *act* in dignified ways. And, happily, that is something over which you have complete control.

Also, make it a point never to use the shopworn excuse "everybody's doing it" to rationalize undignified actions. People who are busy achieving their goals aren't "doing it," whatever "it" may happen to be, for the pragmatic reason that undignified actions simply are not in their best interest. Remember, dignity is about *you*, not society. You can wear your hair purple, put a diamond-studded earring in your nose, and have a snake tattoo burned into your forehead, but no one has to hire you or do business with you. Further, if you decide to go this route, I highly recommend that you not relocate to Singapore, where caning is a national pastime.

The fact is that, in spite of how decadent the world around you may be, you always have the option of rising above the decadence and, as with civility, *commanding* (not *demanding*) the admiration and respect of others through your words and actions.

Finally, keep in mind that silliness is the antithesis of dignified action, so be on guard against people who encourage you to act like a clown—especially if you're invited to appear on *The Tonight Show*. It's a good idea to leave silliness to children.

HONESTY

Honesty is another quality that has given sway to relativism in many quarters during recent times. The lost decade of the sixties moved relativism up to a whole new level, as millions of people felt relieved to discover that lying is not a big deal. When Bill Clinton answered a straightforward question on national television with the almost comedic, truth-twisting line, "It depends upon what the meaning of the word *is* is," he was merely taking the art form practiced by most politicians to its logical extreme.

With this as a backdrop, the fact that numerous polls have found that roughly two-thirds of U.S. students cheat and don't see anything wrong with it is unlikely to change anytime soon. Does anyone seriously believe that an action such as cheating can produce good long-term results for students who not only do it, but see nothing wrong with it?

Call me a Pollyanna, but I think students know better. What they are expressing in these polls is their *desire* to make cheating acceptable. It's a matter of self-delusion, of making true that which they love—and, make no mistake about it, a majority of students love to cheat (or at least love the short-term results of cheating).

Since polls also tell us that the majority of adults regularly lie and, as with students, don't see anything wrong with it, the same self-delusion holds true. So, too, does the reality that they really know better. I agree with C. S. Lewis, who pointed out that, "in our hearts we all know what's right." When two people get into an argument about a dishonest action, the argument is rarely about what is right or wrong; rather, it's usually about *which party* is right or wrong.

So if it's true that we know in our hearts what's right and wrong, why do so many people consistently act dishonestly? The answer lies in that age-old nemesis, instant gratification. A bit of lying here and there can help one to escape a considerable amount of short-term discomfort. The other side of this coin, however, is that dishonest actions almost always lead to *long-term* problems.

I've often heard people say, in response to being caught in a dishonest act, "I had no choice. I had to do it." But they're wrong. You *always* have a choice. It may not be a good choice, but taking honest action is *always* an option. Said Maimonides in the twelfth century, "Any person can become as righteous as Moses or as wicked as Jeroboam. . . . No one forces us, no one decides for us, no one drags us along one path or the other; we ourselves, by our own volition, choose our own way."

We can never escape the reality that, no matter how unpopular it may be, we always have the choice of doing the right thing. And, as with undignified actions, one should never use the lame excuse that "everybody's doing it." The need to be praised by the majority is a sign of insecurity and immaturity. Having the courage to act alone when you know you're in the right is yet another sign of personal growth.

In this regard, one of the most widespread, dishonest acts bred by the everybody's-doing-it culture is computer software theft. You would think that people of this ilk wouldn't feel the need to rationalize stealing from multi-billion-dollar companies. After all, everybody knows that they made their billions by committing the unthinkable crime of creating value for consumers.

Nevertheless, an individual who introduced himself as an avid reader of my books once related to me a fascinating rationalization for stealing software programs, boasting that he possessed a treasure trove of "pirated" copies of programs that friends had made for him. When I pointed out that it is not only illegal to obtain software without paying for it, but immoral as well, he said, "I don't look at it that way. In fact, I think I'm doing a software company a favor when someone gives me a free copy of one of its programs."

With morbid fascination, I asked, "How's that?" Whereupon he replied, "Because if I use the program and like it, I'll tell a lot of other people about it, which results in increased sales for the company." His remark ranked right up there with "That depends upon what the meaning of *is* is." In reality, though, it was just another example of someone making true that which he loved, and this particular person obviously loved to obtain free software.

THE DISHONESTY WEAPON OF CHOICE

Dishonest actions can include such things as stealing, cheating, and deceiving, but in our everyday lives, lying is the form of dishonest action we are most often confronted with. What makes lying so insidious in nature is its many subtle forms.

THE LITTLE WHITE LIE

The little white lie is seemingly innocuous because of its implied harmlessness. A good example of this is when a parent, in an effort to save money, tells a ticket seller at a movie theater that his thirteen-year-old child is only twelve. What's especially bad about this kind of little white lie is that the child makes a mental note of the fact that his parent not only lied, but got away with it. Millions of parents delude themselves about seemingly trivial issues such as this, not thinking of such actions as lying, then wonder why their children turn around and lie to *them*. Such parents attempt to shield their consciousness from the reality that actions have consequences, and that children pay far more attention to what parents *do* than what they *say*.

The problem with little white lies is that the word *little* is subjective; i.e., it has no clear boundaries. This is why little white lies tend to lead to ever greater lies, which in turn lead to increasingly negative long-term results. A lie is a lie regardless of how one tries to label it, so one should never delude oneself into believing that the words *little white* somehow change the nature of the beast.

THE RATIONALIZATION LIE

The rationalization lie is almost always based on self-delusion. Anyone with average intelligence can come up with clever rationalizations for lying. A rationalization lie is usually employed when one is convinced that he has been wronged, the implication being that two wrongs somehow make a right.

As noted in the anecdote I related about software theft, people can become pretty creative when it comes to rationalizing. Isn't lying on your resume just a way of helping a prospective employer make a decision to hire you because you feel certain it would be in his best interest? Isn't inflating your sales figures just a way of making sure that prospective investors don't miss out on the opportunity to invest in your company?

Because so many people go through life feeling as though they are constantly being treated unjustly, they find it easy to rationalize their lies in an effort to "level the playing field." If not curbed early on, however, rationalizations can become the catalyst for an anything-goes philosophy in all areas of one's life.

THE EXAGGERATION LIE

Most people don't think of an exaggeration as a lie, but it is, in every sense of the word. In fact, from a practical standpoint, the exaggeration lie is the most likely kind of lie to be exposed. For this reason, I try to be especially vigilant about not overstating facts. As a writer, you learn (or should learn) early on that the power of the understatement is enormous. Once you catch someone exaggerating, you can't help but downsize all future comments made by him.

If you don't like the idea of people laughing at you behind your back, the best insurance policy against that happening is to not make laughable statements. Understating, rather than overstating, your case is an action that always earns the respect of others.

THE HAIR-SPLITTING LIE

The hair-splitting lie is based on technicalities and is used by people who excel at being clever. To paraphrase economist-historian Thomas Sowell, the problem with being clever is that there is a tendency to try to continue to be clever long past the point where what one has to lose is much greater than what one has to gain. Nothing is more of a turnoff than attempts to be clever by being overly technical even when the facts are clearly against you.

Children are natural masters at the use of hair-splitting lies, and you do them no favor by allowing them to get away with it. Parents repeatedly hear things such as, "I didn't say that I didn't have a *project* to do. I said I didn't have any *homework* to do." Or, "I *didn't* have a detention. The teacher just made me stay after school." It can become exasperating at times, but parents have to stay the course, particularly with adolescents and teenagers, and straighten out such doubletalk early on.

THE OMISSION LIE

The omission lie is the grayest area of lying, because there is always the moral question of which information, and how much information, needs to be divulged at any given time. The best guideline is to ask yourself if the person to whom you are omitting a fact will be negatively impacted by your failure to disclose certain information to him. The omission lie gets right to the heart of honorable intentions. While it's the easiest kind of lie to conceal, it often brings more anger and distrust than any other kind of lie once it is exposed.

THE BIG LIE

The Big Lie is reserved only for professional liars, most people not having the necessary genitalia to attempt it. All the types of lies heretofore mentioned might be likened to a neurosurgeon performing delicate brain surgery with a scalpel, but the Big Lie is more like a lumberjack chopping down a huge tree with an ax—i.e., there is no subtlety about it (e.g., "I did not have sexual relations with that woman"). Amateur liars can't get away with telling the Big Lie, so don't even attempt it if it's just for the thrill of seeing what it feels like. When you tell the Big Lie, you can't be defensive when you get caught; you have to have the genetic makeup to be able to feign indignation and immediately go on the offensive.

Actually, anyone who has mastered the Big Lie shouldn't even be reading this book, because if the Big Lie is the basis for too many of an individual's actions, he is already guaranteed bad consequences throughout his life no matter what else he does right.

INTEGRITY

Integrity is almost synonymous with honesty, but not quite. By definition, integrity is adherence to one's code of moral values or high moral principles. In this respect, it is perhaps more synonymous with consistency. Though people use the word *integrity* quite freely, the world around us suggests that very few really understand what it means, let alone practice it. It's one thing to talk about moral values, but quite another to adhere to them.

A person who consistently acts in accordance with a generally accepted moral code is thought of as *ethical*. A person who preaches a high standard of morality but selectively acts otherwise is thought of as *hypocritical*. A notorious example of hypocrisy would be so-called social-conscience groups that have no qualms about resorting to violence in an effort to further their supposedly goodwill causes.

Because our senses have been so dulled over the past two decades by a seeming tidal wave of acceptable dishonesty, to stay morally on track requires vigilance. It's very easy to be lackadaisical and adopt an everybody's-doing-it attitude. The most certain way to prevent being ensnared by this flimsy excuse is to lay out a clear moral roadmap as early in life as possible (keeping in mind, of course, that later is better than never).

Which means that *you* have to decide what you believe in. *You* have to decide what you believe is moral and what you believe is immoral. *You* have to decide where you want to draw the line on omissions. *You* have to decide if you want to be clever or if you want to be forthright to a fault. You need to have a clear idea of your values ahead of time so you don't base your actions on spur-of-the-moment whims, emotion, or immediate gratification when temptations arise.

The habit of revising one's ethical standards to fit changing circumstances is a practice commonly referred to as "situational ethics." The first step toward acting ethically is to *think* ethically. It's not about "walking the talk"; it's about walking the thought. It's your day-in, day-out thoughts that determine the character of your soul, and one's actions tend to follow one's dominant thoughts.

Integrity demands an answer to this question: How well do you *practice* what you *say* you believe in? Bodhidharma, the sixth-century Zen master, put it simply when he said, "All know the way, but few actually walk it." What he was referring to is something I call *concentricity*—the consistency of one's belief, words, and actions. Think of two perfect circles, one representing what you claim to believe in and what you say, the other representing your actions. When these two circles are almost perfectly aligned, it means you're adhering to your code ethics. On the other hand, if these two circles begin to pull apart, it indicates that you have a problem with your integrity.

Moral slippage initially may seem innocent, reluctant, and/or inconsequential, but almost without exception it tends to mushroom and accelerate. Doesn't the unfaithful spouse often start by cheating on his mate only reluctantly? Doesn't the bank robber usually begin by shoplifting as a youth? Morality is the concept of right and wrong. You either believe that lying, stealing, cheating, and deceiving are right or you believe they are wrong. And if they're wrong, then they are *never* morally justified.

When what you do begins to differ too much from what you claim to believe in and what you say, you'll know something is wrong

CONCENTRICITY

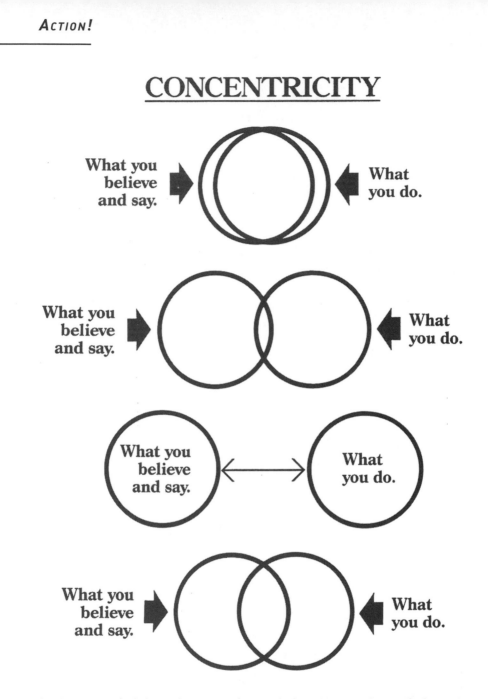

by how you feel deep down inside. And if you're an inherently honest person, it will soon become obvious to you what the problem is.

No one is perfect, so it's not possible for your beliefs and actions to ever coincide perfectly. Which is the very reason you have to be vigilant about striving toward concentricity every day of your life. Such vigilance will lead to consistency in adhering to your values.

We are constantly surrounded by temptations to allow these two circles to pull apart, so it takes a great deal of self-discipline to hold them together. This means avoiding what appear to be quick and easy ways out of bad situations.

Anyone can be honest when it doesn't cause them any inconvenience or discomfort. The true test of your concentricity is when you're faced with a situation where you know that adhering to your moral beliefs might cause you severe pain or embarrassment. That's why you have to think through your moral beliefs ahead of time and be committed to sticking to those beliefs when the going gets tough and the temptations to waver become great.

The simplest way to shore up your concentricity is to live every moment as though the whole world were watching—even in the privacy of your home.

HUMILITY

One of the many wonderful things that our hi-tech, global economy has brought about is the dismantling of corporate arrogance. Pure economics has forced legendarily arrogant companies such as Xerox Corporation and AT&T to come down off their high horses and bend over backward in an attempt to win back customers.

Arrogance usually stems from success-based delusion, whether it be an individual or a corporation. The delusion—or, more properly, self-delusion—I am referring to is the absurd belief that one is indispensable, notwithstanding the fact that history repeatedly teaches us otherwise. Johnny Carson gave way to Jay Leno (and now Leno is about to hand the baton to Jimmy Fallon); Sears Roebuck gave way to Walmart; American-made automobiles gave way to Japanese imports. You could spend all day adding to this list and barely make a dent in the number of well-known examples.

This was brought home to me in dramatic fashion when I was visiting Los Angeles and invited an old friend—an elderly gentleman who had been a big-name television producer—to lunch. I asked him if he was currently working on any projects, to which he gloomily replied, "It's as though I never existed." He went on to explain that a lot of his friends in the industry had died, and others had long ago retired or had their shows cancelled by the networks. Offers no longer found their way to his desk.

My friend's simple comment had a lasting effect on me. The surest way to set negative forces in motion is to start believing you're indispensable. If nothing else, death precludes arrogance, because sooner or later death eliminates everything about which a person has to be arrogant. But long before death, life also does a pretty good job of making a shambles of arrogance.

By contrast, humility is a universally admired virtue. A simple but important truth worth remembering is: *People hate arrogance and love humility.* It's self-evident that you have a leg up in life if people respect and like you rather than disrespect and dislike you. More so than any other virtue, it is all but impossible to fake humility, because what comes out of your mouth immediately places you in your proper slot on the Arrogance-Humility Spectrum in people's minds. This includes *how much* you say, *what* you say, and *how* you say it.

Simple observation tells us that humility and silence go hand in hand. The more truth you discover, the less inclined you are to speak. Speaking exposes one's ignorance, and the wise person knows that his own knowledge is minuscule compared to the infinite wisdom of the universe. Talking is the only action that makes it impossible to learn. The corollary to this is that arrogance and ignorance have a tendency to be cerebral roommates.

There are not many things that can make a person look more foolish than pontificating on a subject he knows little about, a phenomenon commonly referred to as "arrogance of the ignorant." Such childish behavior tends to set the eyes of one's listeners rolling skyward. The surest sign of wisdom is when a person knows enough to know what he does not know. I'm always impressed when someone answers a question with a comment such as, "In all honesty, I'm not well-enough informed in that area to give you a qualified opinion." As a result, when such a person *does* offer an opinion, I place a high value on it.

In the same vein, clearly and promptly admitting you're wrong (when you are) is an almost magical way to gain the respect and cooperation of others. I'm fascinated by people who defend obvious mistakes with a ferocity that leads others to believe that they think they'll be placed in front of a firing squad if they are found to be wrong. Admitting you're wrong is actually a very easy proposition, and each time you do it, it becomes easier than the time before.

GRACIOUSNESS

Graciousness pays big dividends when it comes to human relations. Graciousness is taking the time to return phone calls (or e-mails) even if you don't think the caller currently possesses anything of value to you. When you return calls in a timely fashion, it sets you apart from your ungracious competitors, which usually results in the accumulation and retention of customers.

Graciousness is praising someone for a job well done. Everyone needs reassurance when it comes to his abilities and value. It's not a matter of flattery; rather, it's a matter of being thoughtful enough to speak sincere words of praise when such words are warranted.

Graciousness is taking the trouble to show gratitude to someone who has done you a favor or demonstrated kindness toward you. Showing appreciation for someone's nice gesture is such an easy action to take, yet so rewarding both to you and to the recipient of your thanks. It's a sad commentary on our decadent culture, but a simple display of gratitude is another action that can instantly catapult you to the head of another person's good-guy list.

Graciousness also means not resorting to pettiness. In fact, your Pettiness Meter gives you a pretty accurate reading of where you are in life at any given time. The more a person is mired in frustration and failure, the more willing, even anxious, he is to waste time engaging in petty conversations. When your mind is filled with thoughts of defending yourself, how people have wronged you, and other kinds of petty, cerebral time-wasters, you cannot simultaneously be focused on creative thinking. Your daily energy supply is limited, so it's imperative that you practice converting negative, destructive energy into positive, creative action.

Lastly, graciousness means knowing how to win. The gracious person purposely avoids looking victorious over underlings, peers, and, above all, superiors. There is no easier way to damage relations with others than by being arrogant in victory. Many of the most successful people I know are gracious, polite, and considerate when they accomplish an outstanding feat. It's a great way to make and keep allies with a minimum of effort.

THE BOTTOM LINE: ADDED VALUE

Virtue-based actions translate into added value in the marketplace. When virtues such as those I have discussed in this chapter are evident in an individual, can anyone doubt that he possesses enormous value to a prospective employer or business associate? If you were an employer, do you think you might be interested in hiring someone who is civil, dignified, honest, and humble to a fault?

Even in our age of modern technology, where specialized skills are at a premium, employers always have a place for someone who displays sound virtues. Most skills can be taught, but there's not a lot of interest in the marketplace in teaching people honesty and integrity. Which is why it's wise to have your virtues solidly in place before searching for the right job or approaching someone to become involved with you in a business relationship.

Again, personal growth does not follow achievement; it precedes it. While all actions have consequences, virtue-based actions are those that are most likely to create value for others. And creating value for others is the most gratifying and certain way to achieve success in all areas of life.

CHAPTER 5

People Taxes
and Action

I don't care to belong to any club that would have me as a member.

— GROUCHO MARX

WHILE EVERYONE UNDERSTANDS THAT government taxes—federal, estate, gift, sales, and city, to name but a few—are a fact of life, the heavy burden of people taxes is often overlooked. By *people taxes*, I am referring to the personal resources (such as time, energy, creativity, health, and even wealth) you can waste as a result of allowing the wrong kinds of people into your life. When you suffer a significant loss of these valuable resources, your ability to take action is correspondingly impaired, or "taxed." So people taxes are not taxes *on* action; they are taxes levied by problem people that *hinder* or *prevent* you from taking action.

Government taxes are a minor irritant compared to people taxes because they are confined to a limited number of entities who demand only that you hand over a certain portion of your financial resources to them. People taxes are a much bigger problem, however, because they can be levied, to one extent or another, by virtually every person with whom you come in contact. Additionally, people can assess the same tax over and over again, which means, in extreme cases, that you can end up expending most of your daily efforts just trying to pay your people taxes. Worst of all, people taxes can be levied against your spirit, and when you have to dig into your spirit to pay taxes, your motivation to take action is sure to be impaired.

Thankfully, unlike government taxes, people taxes are voluntary. You have the choice of cutting them off at any time. Yet, most people meekly submit to paying onerous people taxes. Others accept only moderate taxes, and a small percentage of the earth's population opts for minimal people taxation. Obviously, zero taxation is not possible in a world where one has no choice but to come in contact with other people—including problem people—on a regular basis.

If, however, you opt for minimal taxation, the rational way to go about it is to spend less time with people who impose high taxes and more time with those who impose low taxes. The latter would include, for example, individuals who only occasionally engage you in unnecessarily long conversations or irritate you now and then by arguing over a minor point.

Some people are actually net producers rather than net taxers, and, as such, add value to your life; i.e., the value they offer is greater than the amount of personal resources they drain from you. Obviously, to be an action-oriented individual, these are the kinds of people with whom you want to be primarily involved. It's the heavy people taxers—those who assess major taxes against your finite personal resources—who represent a serious obstacle to action.

In addition to draining away personal resources such as time, energy, and creativity, allowing the wrong people into your life also can result in more subtle taxes. One such tax is expressed in the old adage that "you are known by the company you keep." If those closest to you have questionable reputations, your efforts to build a respectable legacy will be for naught. I think most people assume that birds of a feather flock together, and make people judgments accordingly. Can an honest person really be good friends with a notoriously dishonest person? Highly unlikely.

Even worse than being known by the company you keep is that you also tend to *become* like the company you keep. Another old adage warns that you'll never smell like a rose if you roll in a dunghill. This is especially true of children, which is why responsible parents realize that close monitoring of their children's friends is essential until they reach adulthood. Drugs lead to drugs, vulgarity leads to vulgarity, disrespect leads to disrespect. Children are very impressionable, and, as millions of parents have discovered—often too late—they are subjected to intense peer pressure almost daily.

Unfortunately, adults aren't immune to the problem of unconsciously mimicking friends and acquaintances. To some degree, this explains the phenomenon of spouses, in their later years, being so much alike. After thirty or forty years of marriage, how can one not help but adopt much of the thinking and many of the mannerisms of his spouse?

Periodically, then, it's a good idea to step back and think about the people with whom you are spending your time. Where are their words and actions leading you? What thoughts are they influencing you to think? This kind of honest analysis can often lead to shocking revelations about oneself. Better to be shocked, however, than to blindly continue on with relationships that are transforming you into just the kind of person you never wanted to be.

UNDERSTANDING THE TAX COLLECTORS

Realistically speaking, you can't expect to achieve your goals without interacting with, and receiving the help and/or cooperation of, other people. If you start a business, you need to deal with employees, suppliers, customers, regulatory agencies, and many other kinds of people. If you work for someone, you have no choice but to interact with your boss, co-workers, support staff, and anyone and everyone else directly or indirectly related to your job. Whether you play sports (even so-called individual sports), get married and raise a family, or travel the world, people are an integral part of almost everything you do.

Even if you were to attempt to live a Thoreau-type life in the wilderness—a prospect that sounds rather boring—you would find the need to talk to people from time to time. Food and medical care

are two obvious reasons why. That being the case, it makes sense to know as much about human beings as possible. In that vein, a review of some of the more important realities of human nature follows.

IMPERFECTION

We've heard since childhood that no one is perfect, and experience repeatedly confirms the truth in this maxim. We learn this early on when we witness a coach swearing, a teacher punishing us for something we didn't do, or a parent not keeping his word. Nevertheless, from time to time we tend to get so high on someone that we set ourselves up for disappointment. The disappointment often stems from relying too much on the other person; the more we depend on someone, the more likely we are to bring his imperfection to the surface. For this reason alone, striving to be a self-reliant individual can go a long way toward helping you avoid bringing out the worst in people.

SELF-INTEREST

We've already been over this one: *All people are programmed at birth to do what they believe is in their best interests.* To the extent you expect people to act altruistically, you invite unnecessary problems into your life. Keep reminding yourself that you do not have a right to someone's love, friendship, or respect. All these, and more, must be earned. If you choose to act contrary to this principle, the result is likely to be frustration and disappointment. Never forget that the key to getting what you want in life is to focus on actions that create value for others.

RESISTANCE TO CHANGE

People rarely change their personalities or moral structures. Anyone can put on an act for a while, but ultimately the truth will become evident to those who know him. It's important to understand this, because we sometimes go along with a high people tax in the hopes that someone will change his ways. Unfortunately, it rarely happens, which is why it's wise to select business associates, friends, and, most important, spouses on the basis of common values. Opposites may attract, but they tend to end up strangling each other. A marriage between people with conflicting ideologies—i.e., fundamental doctrine that guides their actions—is a perfect example of such a mismatch.

SITUATIONAL ETHICS

Don't expect even the most ethical people to live up to your moral expectations of them 100 percent of the time. All people, at one time or another, deviate from their moral beliefs; i.c., they are sometimes hypocritical. By now you know the lure: instant gratification. Since people are imperfect, you should not be shocked when an otherwise ethical, upstanding friend or acquaintance occasionally engages in situational ethics.

The practice of situational ethics, however, is an unreasonable tax burden when it becomes a way of life for someone—i.e., if it's someone who is in *your* life. If I can never be certain about what a person's ethical stance is going to be from one occasion to the next, I'm likely to spend way too much time thinking about it. Worse, there is an ongoing danger that he might cause me harm whenever I make an assumption about how he's going to handle a given situation.

EASILY IMPRESSED BY MONEY AND POWER

Sadly, most people are impressed by money and power—*especially* those who claim otherwise. Victor Hugo made an astute observation about this reality of human nature when he observed, "Prosperity supposes capacity. Win in the lottery and you are an able man." This reality constantly tests your character. It's also contagious, so you can easily pick it up from others.

The corollary to this trait is that when people think you're broke and powerless, they treat you with indifference, at best; more likely, however, you can count on outright disdain. Remember how the entire office staff ignored my assistant, Joanne, when she was perceived as a low-paid, airhead receptionist? It was fascinating to observe how everyone, after getting over the initial shock of her elevation to the top of the pecking order, began to defer to her judgment on all matters of importance.

SUSCEPTIBILITY TO THE THREE Fs

Most people, regardless of their basic personalities, have the potential to become very ugly when any of the three Fs—fame, fortune, and family—are at stake. Stories of people trampling one another to get to the top of the entertainment ladder are legendary, and anyone with the slightest business experience has witnessed the same kind of ugliness surface when large sums of money are on the line.

Family, however, brings out the most neurotic, ugly behavior of all. This is especially true of parents when they believe their children are being given a raw deal or are in some way being threatened. If you've had any experience coaching Little League baseball or any other kind of youth sports, you know what I'm talking about. A youth coach normally explains to team parents at the start of the season that (1) winning is not important, (2) fun and learning are the team's primary objectives, (3) some children will play more than others, but everyone will play the minimum amount of time required by league rules, and (4) parents should set an example for their children when it comes to good sportsmanship.

All parents assure the coach that they completely understand and agree with everything he has told them, and most of them probably mean it when they give such assurances. In fact, the parents are friendly, gracious, and completely supportive of the coach—the epitome of goodwill—*until the first game of the season*, at which time they begin acting like werewolves in the glow of a full moon.

This neurotic pack of human beasts would be bad enough to take under any circumstances, but heaven help the coach who has a losing season (which is 95 percent determined by the luck of the draft). When that happens, parents who were the most vocal in agreeing that winning is unimportant shed their werewolf costumes and start acting more like prison rioters. If the coach plays his lesser players as little as possible in an effort to turn things around and try to please the win-crazed parents, parents of the children with minimal playing time become hysterical, even threatening the beleaguered coach with physical violence.

Action-Stifling People Taxes

Now that we've reviewed some basic aspects of human nature, let's look at some specific examples of people taxes that are deterrents to action. The people who collect these taxes can include friends and acquaintances, business associates, co-workers, and even spouses or other family members.

THE EVILNESS TAX

I recognize that many people do not believe there is such a thing as evil, and view that which we refer to as evil as merely bad judgment. For our purposes, however, it's not necessary to have an intellectual discussion about whether there is such a thing as pure evil. Instead, I have chosen to loosely define an evil person as someone who enjoys inflicting pain on others and goes about doing it in a premeditated manner.

Having said this, anyone who has ever stared evil in the eye never forgets the moment. You experience a uniquely eerie feeling when talking to an evil person. It's an aura that makes you want to back away. I have no idea why some people are "evil"; I do, however, know that there *are* individuals in this world who enjoy causing others pain. Fortunately, however, they are a small minority.

The danger with evil people is that they are usually very cunning. They wear personality disguises such as joviality, graciousness, and excessive kindness, and have a knack for gathering supporters. They come bearing gifts (politicians?). They tempt you with flattery, and, to the average person unaccustomed to meeting evil, the allure can be irresistible. Most impressive, they are master tellers of the Big Lie. When caught, they quickly take the offensive and try to shame you for questioning their truthfulness. They, in turn, are shameless.

There is a major difference between an evil person and someone who is immoral. All normal people, even if they are immoral, have at least some semblance of a conscience. But in the evil individuals I have encountered, a lack of conscience was the most glaring trait overriding their cunning words and false niceties.

Truly evil behavior is rare, so there is a tendency for people to rationalize it away when they see it, which is exactly how they end up in such places as Jonestown or Nazi concentration camps. While many Jews were unavoidably trapped during Hitler's reign of terror, millions of others deluded themselves into believing that the situation wasn't nearly as threatening as it appeared to be. As a result, they elected not to emigrate from Germany early on when they had the opportunity to do so. Understandably, it was difficult to comprehend the horrors that lay ahead.

While you undoubtedly will never be confronted with such extreme evilness, you will likely experience it in one form or another at some point during your life. Just be prepared and know in advance what to look for; then, when evil does confront you, resist the temptation to rationalize it away. Whatever the cost, move on quickly and absorb any losses that may be necessary. While the temptation may be great, I can promise you that the resulting evilness tax will be more than you can afford to pay.

THE DISHONESTY TAX

It's not difficult to spot dishonesty; the challenge is to do something about it. As with evilness, the tendency is to give people the benefit of the doubt, particularly if their dishonesty is not blatant. This includes individuals who exaggerate, omit material facts, tell little white lies, or regularly engage in situational ethics. All of these acts might seem relatively harmless in a world where dishonesty has become the accepted norm.

But dishonesty is not harmless. If you allow a dishonest person access to your life, and, worse, allow him to overstay his welcome, unnecessary problems are bound to result. As with situational ethics, the main reason for this is that when you're involved with a dishonest person, you can never be certain that you're starting from a correct premise when taking action. When is the person lying, and when is he telling the truth? Again, it's too much to have to think about, too much extra work to have to fit into your already time-scarce schedule.

When someone misleads you—whether it be through exaggeration, omission, or by any other means—the result is likely to be harmful, either to you or to others. At a minimum, you may end up with egg on your face for making bad decisions based on false information, which doesn't do a lot for either your reputation or your dignity. You could liken it to a game of moral Russian roulette: When you act on information supplied by a person who has previously demonstrated a disregard for truth, you never know what you're going to get.

The most shameful type of dishonest person is the prolific hypocrite. As noted earlier, virtually all people are hypocritical to one extent or another, but I'm talking here about extreme cases. The person who makes a pastime of hypocrisy—applying situational ethics on a regular basis—is able to do so because he has no moral obstacles in his path; i.e., because of his amorality, he is free to do just about anything that pleases him at any given moment. This is why it's so important to focus on what people do as opposed to what they say.

Virtually all seriously dishonest people are hypocrites. Hypocrites are often easy to spot by their propensity for giving moral lectures, in many cases heavily seasoned with biblical references. Perverse as it may seem, dishonest people often try to make others believe they are morally superior to them. If you should ever decide that insanity sounds like an appealing way to escape your troubles, an easy method for achieving such a state of mind is to try to get a dishonest person to admit he's dishonest. It simply doesn't happen.

Beware: Once an inherently dishonest person crosses the line and tries to convince you that it's *you* who is dishonest, don't take the bait. Do you really believe that spending inordinate amounts of time trying to convince a dishonest person that you're honest is an efficient way to spend your time? If you haven't had the good sense to have already invited such a person out of your life, his moral accusations are a sure signal that the time has come to do just that—clearly, firmly, and unequivocally. Bad character is malignant; it grows and spreads if not checked early on.

THE DISJOINTED-NOSE TAX

One of the more fascinating experiences of my life with regard to observing human nature occurred about fifteen years ago. A friend had been trying to talk me into hosting a television series on self-development, and had put me in touch with a producer whom he thought would be just right for the project. I wasn't exactly new to the world of dealmaking, so when I spoke to the producer on the phone, I was especially careful to obey all the rules of pragmatic dealmaking—be polite, gracious, and humble; don't talk too much; don't oversell yourself; don't be patronizing; etc. If I behaved all the time as well as I did during that particular telephone discussion, I'd be a candidate for sainthood.

The producer and I talked for about fifteen minutes, and the conversation went extremely well. Before getting off the phone, he told me that he was very excited about the possibility of doing a show with me, and that he would get back to me in a few days to set up a face-to-face meeting. Later that day, my friend called, and I told him how well the conversation with his producer friend had gone.

To my surprise, however, a few days later my friend called again and said, "You're not going to believe this. I just got a letter from the producer I put you in touch with. Want me to read it?"

"Sure," I answered.

He then read, "I'm sorry about the Ringer affair. My chat with him on the phone was *extremely unpleasant*. I figured that if he was going to be so difficult to deal with in a first encounter, the next meeting could only be worse."

To say that I was a bit perplexed would be a wild understatement. Could it be that I had slipped into a trance and made an obscene remark about his mother? I would have searched harder for something I had done wrong, but since nothing like it had ever happened to me before, I suspected that the problem wasn't on my side of the fence. After again assuring my friend that everything about the conversation had been extremely positive, he recalled that on a couple of other occasions he had been told that people had had similar experiences with this particular individual. He said he had not thought much about it before, but that he could now see a pattern.

If you've ever had someone get mad at you for no apparent reason, this little anecdote probably had you nodding your head up and down. So the $64,000 question is, why do some people make a career out of getting mad at the drop of a careless sentence or mis-read facial expression? The answer lies in a simple, eight-letter word: *neurosis*. It is not my job, nor should it be yours, to try to understand what makes a neurotic person tick. This is a serious medical issue, so give yourself a break and let the medical professionals handle it. Why people are neurotic is just one of those great mysteries of life.

It can, however, become a tax burden when a person with this kind of neurosis—someone who always seems to feel slighted or offended for no apparent reason—is consistently in your life. Those who have experienced such a relationship know that it ultimately deteriorates into a game of humoring and tiptoeing in an effort to avoid raising the other person's ire—which translates into an awful lot of wasted effort, not to mention an enormous waste of time.

When someone's nose gets out of joint because you may have said "boo" to him, best you start heading in the opposite direction—unless, of course, you're the curious type. But do remember that curiosity killed the cat.

THE NASTINESS TAX

The disjointed-nose tax results from neurotic individuals who become angry for no apparent reason. The nastiness tax, however, is levied by members of the *Homo sapiens* subspecies known as Nasties, people whose natural personas are just plain sour. Because of their large numbers, and the fact that they are spread over the earth in every imaginable kind of occupation, you have no choice but to come in contact with Nasties from time to time. They are lying in wait for you wherever you do business.

The nastiness tax is most commonly assessed in the world of retail establishments and service businesses—from coffee shops to airlines, from fast-food outlets to offices of all kinds. Unlike most other tax assessors, the reason for the Nasty's nastiness is not a great mystery. Scientists are pretty much in agreement that the cause of every Nasty's demeanor is that he had his favorite rattle taken away from him prematurely during infancy.

"Sorry, I can't take your tray right now, but here's a little hot coffee to help you relax."

Knowing this to be the problem, a sensible objective is to find ways to deal with Nasties that will cause the least amount of disruption to your momentum. This is difficult for someone like me, because I tend to ask a lot of questions, and Nasties absolutely *hate* questions. If you want to witness a Nasty's best growl, try asking a half-dozen questions during any two-minute time span. You will quickly come to find that it's an activity that is dangerous to your health.

Though they are everywhere to be found, Nasties do have their preferred occupations, with airline flight attendant and waiter being at the top of the list. One of the primary qualifications for either job is an "it can't be done" attitude, also known as a bureaucratic mind-set. Did you ever try to hand a flight attendant your tray prior to the designated tray-collection time? Never attempt to do this when the flight attendant is carrying a pot of hot coffee, as your lower body parts may not appreciate the result. Or how about committing a heinous act of aggression, such as asking for a glass of water while the flight attendant is still serving meals?

I try to eliminate such flight-attendant hate crimes by eating before I board a flight—or, if necessary, starving, which is preferable to being on the receiving end of a hot-coffee response. Compassion is in order here, because most flight attendants are nasty as a result of marching in too many picket lines. I feel especially sorry for stewardesses with large calluses on their hands, because it's a dead giveaway that they've had to carry union signs in picket lines a disproportionate number of times.

Waiters, perhaps more than any other kind of retail employees, are notorious for nastiness coupled with a bureaucratic mind-set. A memorable scene from the movie *Five Easy Pieces*, starring Jack Nicholson, highlighted these unpleasant characteristics in a comical way that made it easy for audiences to relate to. Nicholson, playing the character Robert Dupea, was sitting in a diner when a bored and scowling waitress walked up to his booth and asked to take his order. He requested, among other things, a side order of wheat toast, to which the waitress replied, "I'm sorry, we don't have any side orders of toast."

Irritated, Nicholson said, "What do you mean, you don't make side orders of toast? You make sandwiches, don't you? . . . . Okay, I'll make it as easy for you as I can. I'd like an omelet—plain—and a chicken-salad sandwich on wheat toast—no mayonnaise, no butter, no lettuce—and a cup of coffee."

Increasing the intensity of her scowl, the waitress repeated the order, then asked, "Anything else?"

Nicholson responded, "Yeh, now all you have to do is hold the chicken, bring me the toast, give me a check for the chicken-salad sandwich, and you haven't broken any rules."

"Okay, Ms. Nice, I'll make it as easy for you as I can. I want a lox and bagel sandwich—no lettuce, no tomato, no cream cheese. Hold the lox, bring me the bagel, and give me a check for the lox and bagel sandwich."

The screenwriter's clever words in *Five Easy Pieces* magnified the absurdity of the waitress's nasty, bureaucratic attitude. However, even though Jack Nicholson's little diatribe was a film classic, my experience with Nasties has convinced me that it's a bad idea to be confrontational when dealing with them—especially in the case of waiters. The thought of what the waiter or cook might put in my food to exact retribution for my insubordination is enough to steer me away from confrontations.

To the extent you can't avoid Nasties—and avoidance *should* always be your first line of defense—I strongly suggest that you learn the art of humoring them. For example, when a scowling, bureaucratic post office employee makes some absurd statement about why he can't accommodate a simple request, learn to bite your mental lip and say something like, "Gee, I didn't know that. Thanks for telling me; I'll sure keep it in mind from now on. You seem to be someone who knows how to get things accomplished (a preposterous comment that almost always works), so perhaps you could suggest a way that we could make this happen. Do you think it might work if we . . . ?" (Then give him the solution in a way that makes it sound like it's *his* idea.)

You can never totally remove Nasties from your life, so the art of humoring is an essential tool for handling them. Though I am generally against humoring people, because it's a subtle form of dishonesty, in the case of Nasties I consider it to be more a matter of self-defense. The only other solution I know of is to carry a concealed weapon, but is it really worth life in prison just to rid the world of one Nasty?

THE NEGATIVISM TAX

Though you yourself may possess a positive outlook on life, it's still a bad idea to be around negative people, particularly those who are negative about your aspirations or goals. Even if you try to ignore negativism in your midst, spoken words (not to mention facial expressions) are recorded by your subconscious mind. Just as positive images stimulate your body mechanisms to do whatever is necessary to convert those images into physical realities, so it is with negative images, which explains the phenomenon of "self-fulfilling prophecies." Negative images are surefire action stoppers.

Whatever course of action you may choose, there will always be someone close at hand who is more than happy to tell you why you're making a mistake. If you allow too much negativism to enter your subconscious mind—let alone your conscious mind—when difficulties arise, it's quite natural to begin wondering if your critics weren't right after all.

Aside from attacking your personal goals, some people are just negative about life in general. Life loves to beat you down, but you have no obligation to help it do so. Because life offers plenty to be negative about, that's all the more reason to avoid negative people. You need all the positive thoughts you can absorb in order to combat the never-ending stream of unpleasantness that invites itself into your life. In extreme cases, a negative thought can nudge a person from frustration to despair, and despair can rapidly become a terminal problem.

Further, remember that you have to deal with nasty people and bureaucrats throughout life, and they will gladly provide you with all the negativism you can handle. Virtually all nasty people and bureaucrats are negative, but not all negative people are nasty or bureaucratic. Which is precisely why negativism can sneak up on you before you realize the impact it's having on your thoughts. Some of the nicest people I know are negative, which in some respects makes them potentially more dangerous than negative people who are nasty. When it comes to nastiness, you're usually on guard, but you tend to let down your guard when you're in the presence of a pleasant person.

In fact, the Negativism Tax is often levied by those closest to you, particularly family members, so it can be an especially difficult tax to cope with. The friend or family member offering "advice" may be well meaning, but his observations could still be incorrect. Because of this danger, you should condition yourself to make tough decisions when it comes to not allowing even the nicest negative people to come into, or stay in, your life. If you need inspiration to accomplish this, just ask yourself how many times you've achieved successful results when you were in a negative state of mind.

Criticism is a specific form of negativism. There's nothing wrong with constructive criticism, provided it comes from the right party. By *right party*, I'm talking about people whom you respect and who truly have your best interests at heart, in which case it would be more proper to refer to their comments as "constructive advice." Constructive advice from the right party can be worth a fortune to you over the long term, while ill-intended criticism from the wrong party can do more to tear you down, damage your self-esteem, and prevent you from actively pursuing your dreams than just about anything else I can imagine.

As such, it's important to be selective about the people from whom you accept criticism. Do you respect the person handing out the criticism? Are his own hands clean with regard to the subject matter of his criticism? Does he have his own life in order? If the answers to any of these questions are *no*, thank the person for his "concern," then simply delete his comments from your mind.

Unfortunately, some people cannot be happy unless they are successful in converting others to conform to their ways. While continually chastising you for not changing, they never consider that you may not want to change, that you actually like your life just fine the way it is. And it certainly never crosses their minds that you may find *their* way of life to be unappealing.

The agendas of some people seem to be nothing more than to discourage others, preferably by assuring them that they can't succeed at what they're trying to accomplish. If there's one thing you don't need in your life, it's someone who emphasizes negatives and tries to chip away at your self-confidence. Unfortunately, we live in a very negative world, and we don't have to look very far to find someone who is more than willing to tell us why our objectives are unattainable.

A pathological critic usually is just an unhappy person who repeatedly confirms the truth in the old saying "misery loves company." Such an individual thrives on the opportunity to pull others down to his level, and, if you're not careful, he can soon have you prostrating yourself and relating your troubles to him. At that point, he's got you. He will happily pontificate to you, appoint himself as your psychologist, and tell you everything that's wrong with you—with a certitude that implies that he is problem-free and totally well adjusted. His ultimate joy is to succeed in making *you* psychologically dependent upon *him*.

In this regard, be especially wary of so-called experts, especially self-anointed experts whose chief objective seems to be to make certain that you clearly understand their superiority over you. Bold action is the quickest and most certain way to neutralize an expert—or any critic, for that matter—because the whole objective of a negative person is to *prevent* others from taking action. Action is the initial step when it comes to getting results, and results make negativists look and feel impotent.

Writers learn about negativism early on, because they are criticized regularly by total strangers, particularly book reviewers. Ignoring professional critics isn't an act of defiance; it's a matter of survival. A writer would have to be suicidal to base his work on the opinions of a handful of critics. In this regard, two quotes have been enormously helpful to me over the years, preventing me from allowing my philosophy and writing style to be altered by critical comments. The first, which I read every morning before sitting down to write, is from E. B. White: "The whole duty of a writer is to please and satisfy himself, and the true writer always plays to an audience of one." The second is from Ayn Rand: "Freedom comes from seeing the ignorance of your critics and discovering the emptiness of their virtue."

In substance, however, these two quotes apply to everyone, not just writers. It is both admirable and noble to believe in your work and your code of ethics strongly enough to be able to ignore uninvited criticism. I'm sure that you don't need me to remind you that to the degree you are successful, you *will* be criticized, because success breeds jealousy and envy. To paraphrase the late 19th century essayist Elbert Hubbard, the only way to escape criticism is to say and do nothing, which, in turn, guarantees that you will accomplish nothing. Constructive advice can be of great value, but ill-intended criticism from the wrong party can become a huge obstacle to action.

THE RUDENESS TAX

When it comes to not returning phone calls, which is number one on my pet-peeve list when it comes to rudeness, Rude Mongers usually invoke the excuse that they've been too busy, which I personally find insulting, for two reasons.

First, when someone tells me how busy he's been, he is at least implying that he doesn't think I'm busy. I can't imagine anyone busier than I am, but I always find time to return phone calls. That's because I assume that everyone who calls me is busy, too.

Second, when a person says that he's been too busy to return your phone call, what he's really telling you is that you're not a high priority on his "to do" list. And when it comes to business, in particular, that's a bad posture from which to operate.

Rather than pursue a better opportunity with someone who repeatedly shows, through his actions, that I'm a low priority with him, I would much rather deal with someone who offers me less opportunity but *demonstrates* that he considers me to be a top priority. An action-oriented individual simply doesn't have time to sit and wait for someone to get around to calling him back.

Aside from the enormous waste of time and energy, an even better reason for making short shrift of rude people is that they can be extremely damaging to your self-esteem. Can there be anything more degrading than chasing after someone who is rude and disrespectful to you? You have every right to expect the same politeness from others that you show to them. One-sided relationships are always a bad idea.

I find that rude people are a heavy burden on my time and energy resources. While you can't force someone to treat you with respect—i.e., it's not a "right"—it *is* your right to decide whom to keep out of your life. So when dealing with Rude Mongers, it's important to learn the art of saying "Next!"

THE OBLIGATION TAX

The Obligation Tax arises when someone unilaterally decides that you have an obligation to him. In business, this often takes the form of an abstract phenomenon commonly referred to as a "lost opportunity." I use the word *abstract*, because a lost opportunity is impossible to quantify, yet it's a staple of people who are obligation-taxers.

My most memorable experience with the obligation tax occurred in New Zealand when I was searching for a full-time sales and motivational trainer to work with my company's distributors. An acquaintance in Sydney had submitted a number of names to me for consideration, and I subsequently requested resumes from the people who appeared to be the most qualified. I finally narrowed the list down to two individuals, one female and one male, and flew each of them to New Zealand for an interview.

I explained to the candidates that I did not want to make any long-term commitment until I had the opportunity to see them in action, particularly given the draconian reality in New Zealand that a job is an asset of the employee. I agreed to pay each a substantial fee for spending a week in New Zealand and conducting training sessions, and told them that I would then evaluate their performances and let them know if I was interested in pursuing a more permanent relationship.

As it turned out, I decided against hiring either of these people, not because I wasn't impressed with their skills, but because I wasn't certain the "chemistry" was right. I telephoned the female trainer first, explained my position, and told her that I would like to keep in touch and possibly use her services in the future on a consulting basis. She was very cordial, and said that she looked forward to working with me again.

I then called the male trainer and told him pretty much the same thing, but his response was quite different. He went into a tirade about how he had sold his interest in a promising venture for the express purpose of going to work for my company, and how he was now left out in the cold by my not hiring him. After reminding him of the conditions I had originally outlined, I asked him how he could now be worse off than he was before his one-week New Zealand tour.

In response, he railed on and on about his "lost opportunity." He was now much worse off, he said, because he could have "had it made" had he stuck with the project he was involved in for more than a year before I had contacted him. (It's interesting to point out that he never explained why he would walk away from such a lucrative opportunity in the first place.) It was, of course, pure nonsense, but a vivid reminder of how some people will not hesitate to try to saddle even relative strangers with obligations created in their own minds.

The "lost opportunity" is the ultimate manufactured obligation, and the person who engages in it is likely to be telling his grandchildren thirty years down the road how he would have been fabulously wealthy had some malevolent person not caused him to lose out on the opportunity of a lifetime. When someone gripes about your being the cause of a lost opportunity for him, don't buy into it. His hurt feelings will eventually heal, and, who knows, perhaps he will then make a commitment to take responsibility for his own actions.

THE IRRATIONALITY/IGNORANCE TAX

A brilliant attorney once told me that he would rather do battle with a smart, unethical attorney than one who was ethical but irrational or ignorant. He said the problem was that there was no way to communicate his arguments to an irrational or ignorant attorney; i.e., regardless of how logical and factual his points might be, his counterpart would be intellectually incapable of processing them.

While irrationality may in part be due to genetics, it is a trait that tends to get worse as an individual's personal circumstances deteriorate. For example, a person may be born with a tendency to blame others for his problems, but as his problems multiply, he will tend to increase his efforts to look elsewhere for the source of his troubles—which, of course, only makes his problems worse. As a result, he becomes entrapped in a vicious cycle.

To a great extent, the same is true of ignorance. Genetics, of course, plays a major role here, but keep in mind that ignorance is not the same as stupidity. Stupidity stems from a lack of mental capacity, i.e., naturally slow thinking, or "dullness." Ignorance results from an inferior knowledge base. In essence, a search for truth is a search for knowledge, so if an individual repeatedly fails in his search for truth, he will appear ignorant to knowledgeable people. The cause of an individual's ignorance may stem from a lack of education (not necessarily formal education) or simply from being taught, and accepting, too many falsehoods.

The reason I have grouped irrationality and ignorance together is that dealing with either of these conditions yields pretty much the same results. You can't reason with an irrational person, because he lacks sound reasoning powers. And you can't reason with an ignorant person, because he lacks the knowledge necessary to understand what you're talking about. Since you are unable to employ reason in either case, whether a person is irrational or ignorant becomes a moot point. Either way, he is eminently capable of wasting your time.

There is, however, one significant difference between someone who is irrational and someone who is ignorant. An ignorant person simply doesn't know the facts, but an irrational person's problem is usually that he is self-delusive. That means he possesses the ability to ignore facts, which, in turn, blinds him from the truth. He simply blocks out any information that contradicts his faulty belief system and tenaciously clings to his erroneous version of reality.

This was true of my friend Jeremy, who employed self-delusion to rationalize his cult activities. He had the capacity to discuss most subjects—i.e., those that posed no danger to his cult beliefs—in impeccably rational terms, yet he would become almost maniacally irrational when it came to discussing any topic that threatened to undermine his justifications for his cult activities.

In theory, an ignorant person with reasonable intelligence can be taught the truth, but is that really how you want to spend your life? Unless you're a professional teacher, you would have to place a very high value on someone to invest a significant amount of your limited time resources trying to educate him. When it comes to educating others, children are a full-time job for most people. For this reason alone, you should think long and hard before trying to educate a nonfamily member without compensation. A much more sensible idea is to focus your energy on cultivating relationships with rational, well-informed people who are not burdensome.

THE DEBATE TAX

The debate tax can be the most exhausting of all people taxes. By the term *debate*, I am referring to the act of arguing, disputing, or contesting. An argumentative person is not only unpleasant to be around, but he also can consume large chunks of your time—time that could otherwise be used in beneficial ways. It's true that an irrational or ignorant person can also be a relentless debater. However, the added tax threat that such a person poses as a result of his penchant for debating is a moot point, because his irrational behavior is enough reason, of and by itself, to keep him out of your life.

An accomplished, incurable debater has the potential to frustrate and exhaust you to a degree only dreamed of by other kinds of people taxers. Whether or not you believe you are capable of out-debating someone should never be the issue. The real issue is: Why in the world you would even care to try? Earlier, I suggested that if insanity sounded like an appealing way to escape your troubles, an easy method for achieving such a state of mind would be to try to get a dishonest person to admit he's dishonest. In the same vein, another way to achieve insanity is to spend a great deal of your time trying to debate an irrational person.

Because relationships with debaters have such great potential for slowing you down, it's important to be able to recognize when you're in close proximity to such an individual. To help toward that end, I have summarized below the Ten Dirty Tricks of Debating, which are the most commonly used tools of the debater's trade.

DIRTY TRICK #1: THE FALSE PREMISE
Basing one's argument on a false premise is one of the oldest tricks of clever debaters. It's a mainstay of most political debates, wherein politicians find that they can slide a false premise by sitcom-damaged brains without much effort. Worse, supposedly opposing parties (as in, Democrats and Republicans—or, more appropriately, *Demopublicans*) begin most of their debates with joint false premises, thus giving viewers all the more reason to assume that such premises are correct.

DIRTY TRICK #2: USING THE DESIRED CONCLUSION AS A PREMISE

Using the desired conclusion as a premise—sometimes referred to as an *a priori* argument—is just a bold version of basing one's arguments on a false premise. The debater who employs this tactic merely restates his own conclusion as though it were a fact.

DIRTY TRICK # 3: PUTTING A SPIN ON A NEGATIVE

The term *spin* refers to the art of cleverly and smoothly twisting the truth, and it is now considered an essential tool for those who have dedicated their lives to the art of debating. The objective is to take a crystal-clear fact that negatively affects the spinner and twist it—i.e., "put a spin on it"—in such a way that it gives the illusion of being a positive.

DIRTY TRICK #4: FEIGNING INDIGNATION WHEN TRAPPED

Some people are world-class actors when it comes to feigning indignation in situations where they realize they've been caught in a lie, misstatement, or worse. I have a simple rule when it comes to indignation: The louder and more vehement the protest, the less credence I give to the person's indignation. As Emerson put it, "You shout so loudly I can barely hear your words."

DIRTY TRICK #5: TAKING THE OFFENSIVE WHEN OVERWHELMED BY THE FACTS

Taking the offensive with an aggressive, all-out attack is a strategy that goes a step beyond just feigning indignation, and is often employed when the facts appear to be undermining one's arguments. The more overwhelming the facts against the dirty-trick debater, the more aggressive he becomes and the more effective he is in getting the other party to back off.

DIRTY TRICK #6: MAKING INTIMIDATING ACCUSATIONS

Making intimidating accusations is another trademark of political debaters, the objective being to put the other party on the defensive. Some popular accusations, both in and out of the political arena, include: "You're just selfish"; "You don't care about starving children"; and, the ultimate intimidating accusation, one that quickly brings most people to their apologetic knees, "You're a racist."

DIRTY TRICK #7: FOCUSING ON IRRELEVANT POINTS

Switching the focus of the conversation is a convenient way to escape being overwhelmed by the truth. Straying from the main point and changing the subject is a dead giveaway that the facts are closing in on the debater. Criminal defense attorneys employ this art when they distract the jury's attention from any damning evidence against their clients by focusing on side issues and irrelevant topics.

DIRTY TRICK #8: USING INVALID ANALOGIES

Oversimplified, an invalid analogy is the equivalent of comparing apples to oranges. When a debater uses an analogy, you have to follow his words carefully and make certain that *A* matches up with *B* and *C* matches up with *D*, or you'll find yourself boxed into a corner. If you allow an invalid analogy to slip by uncontested, you're heading toward its natural consequence—an invalid conclusion.

DIRTY TRICK #9: DEMANDING PROOF FOR A SELF-EVIDENT FACT

There is a whole school of thought that revolves around the idea that everything is relative and therefore nothing can be proved. The philosophy of relativism teaches that the premises people use to make judgments vary according to their genetic makeup, backgrounds, and environments. However, an axiom is a self-evident truth that requires no proof, and rational, honest people do not require proof for self-evident truths. You do not have to prove that the sun comes up each morning, but there was a time when it was necessary to prove that the earth revolved around the sun. As with invalid analogies, if you allow someone to base his argument on the contention that a self-evident truth cannot be proven, an invalid conclusion is also a forgone conclusion.

DIRTY TRICK #10: USING INTELLECTUAL OR ESOTERIC WORDS
While esoteric language makes for good entertainment, you should never allow someone to use it against you in a debate. I am an advocate of Occam's Razor Principle (also known as the Principle of Parsimony), which states that the simplest and most direct explanation is generally the best explanation. Making explanations more complicated than necessary is often nothing more than a smokescreen intended to hide the facts.

No matter which of the above dirty tricks is employed, the bottom line is that you can't afford to waste time on people who turn every conversation into a debate. You must learn to rise above the fray, and the best way I know to do that is to ask yourself if the resolution of a point of contention is really all that important in the overall scheme of things. With very few exceptions, the answer is *no*. A debater becomes impotent if he has no one with whom to debate, and you should make it a point never to volunteer to reinstate his virility. If you aspire to an action-filled life, you don't have time to be constantly debating anyone.

LOWERING YOUR PEOPLE TAXES

In addition to those I have discussed in this chapter, there are numerous other personality traits that can be quite taxing, so lowering your people taxes can be a daunting task. However, keep in mind that there are no perfect human beings, so just because someone possesses one or more unappealing traits does not necessarily mean he is a high tax burden on you. The focus of this chapter has been on extreme cases—those people who have the emotional tools to drain you of so much time and energy that they become obstacles to your taking action toward achieving your goals.

Remember, unlike government taxes, people taxes are voluntary, so it's up to you to decide what the amount of your people taxes will be. You can live an action-oriented life or you can pay excessive people taxes, but you can't do both; clearly, they are mutually exclusive. With that in mind, I have listed below some recommendations that I believe will help you in keeping your people taxes to a minimum.

DON'T DELUDE YOURSELF

Earlier, I cautioned against giving dishonest people the benefit of the doubt, and to a great extent that advice is applicable when it comes to all people taxers. It's human nature to want to believe the best about others, which is why we tend to make so many mistakes when it comes to judging people.

However, the reality is that you don't have enough hours left in your life to give proper attention to those you already know to be worthy, so why stretch your boundaries to become involved with marginal people? It's far better to trust your instincts and err on the side of caution. I find that with each passing year my instincts about people improve and, as a result, I'm ever more inclined to heed the ancient proverb that warns, "You must have gold to make gold."

As previously noted, it's important to learn to differentiate between speech and actions. It's not what people say but what they do that counts. There is much wisdom in another proverb that states, "Your ears are to hear only what your eyes miss."

Likewise, don't allow money or power to sway your judgment. Some of the biggest people taxers I've encountered were rich and powerful. As I said earlier, people tend to be impressed by money and power, so such situations are a good test of your character. Seneca alluded to this when he warned, "A man who examines the saddle and bridle and not the animal itself when he is out to buy a horse is a fool; similarly, only an absolute fool values a man according to his clothes or his position, which after all are things we wear like clothing."

The most prudent guideline to follow for judging a potential people taxer is: *When in doubt, keep him out.* Don't delude yourself into believing that people will change; they won't. Instead, cut your losses short and remove action-killers from your path as quickly as possible. A piece of wisdom handed down over the generations from an unknown source cautions, *Never get in a lifeboat with a cannibal.* Maybe it's my fear of being transformed into turtle soup that keeps me on my toes when it comes to assessing people.

"Could I interest you in our debating special, my little green friend?"

NEVER CONFUSE GOOD INTENTIONS WITH BAD CONSEQUENCES

A sad reality about people taxes is that individuals with good intentions can sometimes tax you as much or more than those who have bad intentions. People often make remarks such as, "But he means well." Maybe it's just me, but I don't understand how to interpret "means well." Does it mean that someone should be allowed to sap your time and energy resources because he has good intentions?

This is when the going can get really sticky, because it often means making tough decisions about friends, spouses, or other family members. A spouse who continually berates you for pursuing your dreams is a classic example of someone close to you who can derail your best-laid plans.

It still amazes me how many letters I have received throughout my career from people who have told me that they parted ways with a spouse or domestic partner after reading one of my books, almost always resulting in a better life for them. This used to make me feel uncomfortable, but after rechecking my premises I began to feel good about the fact that I had helped so many people find happier, more fulfilling lives.

Don't for a second think that I'm making light of divorce, but spending a lifetime with a person who makes every minute of your existence unpleasant is a far worse alternative than enduring the pain of a divorce.

NEVER TRY TO FIGURE OUT THE OTHER PERSON'S NEUROSIS

Yet another activity that can lead to insanity is attempting to figure out the cause of someone's actions. You're better off simply classifying a people-taxer's actions as just irritations that are beyond human understanding, then moving on to more productive matters. Whenever I have an encounter with someone who is rude, negative, irrational, or just plain neurotic, I enter it into the passive-fascination compartment of my brain, then forget about it.

Passive fascination with people's traits and actions is a harmless thought process, but if you allow your fascination to become active, you open the door to some potentially high people taxes. Again, it's a job for those in the psychiatric field who get paid to be actively fascinated. Be humble enough to admit that you have absolutely no idea why neurotic individuals act the way they do—and let it go at that.

DON'T TRY TO CHANGE PEOPLE

Feeling compelled to change others is the height of arrogance. At least one of the reasons why there is so much hate and war in the world is that so many people feel morally obliged to remake people in their own image. Even if such a lofty objective were moral (which it isn't), it would be impossible, which is why force is always used in the pursuit of such an objective. This ugly reality has been a fact of life since the beginning of recorded history, and, if anything, is worse today than ever before.

Earlier in this chapter, I listed as one of the realities of human nature the fact that people rarely change their basic personalities or moral structures, noting that we sometimes go along with a high people tax in the hopes that a person will change. In those rare instances where significant change does occur, it almost always comes from personal revelation rather than through the efforts of someone else.

Selecting the right kind of people to be in your life is a whole lot easier than opening the door to the wrong people in the first place, then trying to change them. And if a high people taxer has already managed to sneak into your life, it's a lot less expensive, not to mention less painful, to evict him than it is to undertake the near impossible, time-consuming, frustrating task of trying to change him.

ALWAYS CONTROL THE SITUATION

When it comes to people taxes, it's important to be proactive rather than reactive. *You* should decide whom you want in your life, then take appropriate action if adjustments are necessary. Basically, you have only two options when it comes to ridding yourself of a people tax being levied by someone in your life.

The first option is to humor the person and avoid him as much as possible, which really is just a method of postponing the inevitable and prolonging your discomfort. The second option is to completely eliminate the person from your life, which is a *permanent* solution. It's almost always a good idea to confront a problem head on and get it over with.

Elimination may be unpleasant in the short term, but, if properly handled, the long-term benefits can last a lifetime. Just keep in mind that a people problem is likely to remain in your life until *you* take action.

If you ask the offending party for his opinion on how best to resolve what you perceive to be a problem with your relationship (meaning a problem in *your* life), you can count on losing control of the situation. Since the other person is an obstacle to your ability to take goal-oriented action, the last thing in the world you want to do is ask *his* opinion on how best to go about removing that obstacle.

ALWAYS REMEMBER HOW THE king's wise men summed up all the wisdom in the world in one sentence. There is no free lunch when it comes to personal relationships any more than there is with financial matters. This is why the fewer favors you ask of people, the less likely you are to be disappointed.

For all practical purposes, the supply of people who can add value to your life is unlimited. But if your desire is to be associated with decent people, you must be prepared to pay a decent price. Specifically, you should be prepared to add value to the lives of those people with whom you want to be involved.

Also, keep in mind that time is a limiting factor when it comes to finding people who can add value to your life, which is a good reason why you should waste as little time as possible on those individuals who offer only problems. That, in turn, leaves you with more time to spend on finding quality people who have the potential to be net producers rather than net taxers.

Taxes lead to pain; added value leads to pleasure. Luckily, you have the power to choose between the two. Make it a habit to focus on associating with people who make it easier for you to take action, and disassociate yourself from people who have a knack for slowing you down.

CHAPTER 6

Freedom and Action

The first halting step toward freedom of the self is the acknowledgement of one's enslavement.

— GERRY SPENCE

FREEDOM GOES HAND IN hand with action, because if you're not free to take action toward pursuing your dreams and achieving your goals, you are, metaphorically speaking, a slave. Slaves are not free to act in their own best interests.

People often feel imprisoned by such things as marriage, work, financial pressures, and just everyday stress, to name but a few of the more commonly expressed freedom thieves. Even the most seemingly innocent annoyances—such as housework, household repairs, employees (if you're a business owner), school events, having to shave every morning, too many houseguests, or simply too many commitments—can make you feel constrained to the point of frustration and despair.

People talk endlessly about freedom, but rarely take the trouble to examine its roots. Freedom begins with a concept called *Natural Law*.

The underlying premise of Natural Law is that every individual owns his own life, and for that reason possesses the right to do whatever he desires with that life so long as he does not forcibly interfere with the life of any other person. Many people, of course, do not agree with the underlying premise of Natural Law, particularly those who want to be free to curb the freedom of others. This is what most political action groups are about.

If, however, one agrees with the premise of Natural Law, he is also compelled to agree that no one has the authority to grant natural rights to anyone else, because human beings already possess all natural rights at birth. These natural rights include both personal and economic freedoms, and the only way they can be lost is if someone takes them away by force.

While virtually everyone claims to be in favor of freedom, there is much disagreement about what freedom really means. One person's idea of freedom might mean his being able to do whatever he wants to do with his own life, while another person's idea of freedom might mean (and often does mean) his being able to do whatever he wants to do with other people's lives. And you can be certain that, given the opportunity, such a person is going to see to it that your actions are in *his* best interest rather than yours.

FREEDOM FROM

Even though every inhabitant of our planet is to one extent or another enslaved by governments, people in so-called democratic societies are relatively free to take action to better their lives. Thankfully, while we can do little about the areas of our lives controlled by government, the majority of things in our day-to-day lives by which we feel most enslaved are those we have the power to control. Specifically, I'm talking about obstacles that get in the way of our taking action, but from which we can free ourselves if we so choose. Some of the more important of these obstacles are discussed in the remainder of this chapter, and gaining freedom in these areas is attainable by virtually any person who is determined not to settle for less.

FREEDOM FROM THE PAST

Who among us does not have unpleasant experiences in his past? Being bullied in school, getting cut from an athletic team, losing a sweetheart to a rival, the premature death of a parent, failing a licensing exam, or suffering through an ugly divorce are the kinds of painful experiences that stay with most people throughout life. Some things we're ashamed of, others we're angry about. But whatever our emotions about the past may be, they clog the gears of our brains and prevent us from moving forward with life in a positive, constructive way.

The inability to let go of the past is a self-imposed imprisonment, an imprisonment from which only you can free yourself. Being imprisoned by the past often involves dwelling on some great injustice one has suffered. The problem of injustice is discussed in detail in Chapter 8, but let it suffice to say here that you have two options when it comes to dealing with injustice. You can allow it to destroy the remainder of your life or you can use it as a motivating force to accomplish great things.

An important aspect of letting go of the past is to continually remind yourself that despite the level of success you may have achieved, the past is etched in stone and can never be changed. If so, there is no rational reason for allowing it to destroy your future as well. The more you intellectualize these self-evident truths, the more likely they are to be adopted, through mental osmosis, by the emotional cells of your brain. This is similar to the concept of positive visualization—holding an image in your mind and thereby stimulating your body's mechanisms to do whatever is necessary to convert that image into its physical reality.

Another important intellectual aspect of letting go of the past is to refuse to use the word *but*. "I know it's not healthy for me to continue thinking about how I got shafted in that deal, *but* I just can't stop" is a commonly heard type of response to the problem of letting go of the past. Or, "I know I can't do anything about it now, *but* if he had given me the opportunity, I would be in a different position today." The variations are endless, but the essence is always the same: In each and every case, *but* is used as a crutch to hang on to the past.

But is a word children should be encouraged to use as little as possible, because it's the starting point for the destructive practice of blaming others—which, in turn, is the gateway to failure. *But* is the most convenient escape hatch for the individual intent on avoiding personal responsibility. More often than not, when you eliminate the word *but*, you eliminate the excuse itself. Instead of relying on *but*, practice saying things such as, "I know it's wrong to think about the past, *so I'm going to stop*" or "I know I can't do anything about it now, *which is why I'm going to forget about it.*"

Freedom from the past is essential to an action-oriented life. If your mind is cluttered with stressful thoughts about the past, paralysis tends to set in, and action dies. The only contribution the past can make to your future is through the experience it has given you, and it's up to you to convert that experience into wisdom. The future lies on the other side of the prison door of the past, a door you possess the power to open and step through at any time. That step is one of the most important actions you can ever take.

FREEDOM FROM PERFECTION

In absolute terms, of course, there is no such thing as perfection. Therefore, perfection is an unobtainable goal, and an unobtainable goal is destined to result in frustration. An obsession with perfection produces action-suffocating stress and thereby becomes an enemy of action. However, perfection is a two-edged sword. While it's impossible for human beings to attain perfection, taking pride in one's work and *striving* for perfection is a noble way to live one's life. The aphorism about moderation being the best policy is particularly applicable when it comes to perfection.

ONE OF THE MOST COSTLY kinds of perfection is overpreparation. Preparation is a good thing, but, as with perfection in general, overpreparation is anathema to action. There's a fine line between being *well* prepared and *over*prepared.

In this regard, the invention of the modern computer, particularly the laptop, has served as a drug for overpreparation addicts. You see them on every flight, diligently punching numbers into their little spreadsheets and going to extremes to make them as detailed and fancy-looking as possible. Perhaps even worse are the PowerPoint addicts. Before the advent of today's software, most of these guys produced documents so sloppy they would embarrass a sixth grader, but today everyone can create beautiful spreadsheets and PowerPoint presentations.

While I suppose there are exceptions, my personal experience has been that a significant number of those who are laptop preparation addicts seldom get around to implementing their plans. I can't tell you how many bad experiences I've had with people who are addicted to spreadsheet projections and PowerPoint presentations. Days roll into weeks, weeks into months, and months into years—and they just keep working away on their laptops.

These Laptopians are incurably addicted to their little perfection machines, and, worse, on those rare occasions when one of their business models is actually put to the test in the real world, their projections rarely prove to be within shouting distance of how things actually play out. The only way that a Laptopian can be absolutely certain of at least one thing being right in his spreadsheet or PowerPoint presentation is to put a bold statement at the top of his masterpiece that proclaims: **I HEREBY GUARANTEE THAT I WILL BE COMING BACK TO YOU FOR MORE CAPITAL—MUCH MORE CAPITAL—SHORTLY AFTER YOU GIVE ME MY INITIAL FUNDING.**

I've been involved in some remarkable deals that were outlined on the back of a napkin over dinner.

IN EXTREME CASES, AN obsession with perfection can completely negate your efforts, which is precisely what happened to me with a project I worked on in the late nineties. After years of poking around in WordPerfect just enough to get by, I reluctantly came to the conclusion that if I wanted to speed up my word-processing output, I was going to have to invest the time to gain a more in-depth understanding of the program.

Meanwhile, my assistant, Joanne, had been trying to get me to switch to Microsoft Word. However, like most people who know just enough to barely get by on a computer, I was insecure about letting go of the one software program in which I was minimally proficient.

Finally, with considerable apprehension, I decided to go along with Joanne's recommendation, and we switched all our office computers to Microsoft Word. What helped push me over the line were her assurances that all I would need was a good Word reference guide and I'd be up and running in no time. I actually ended up buying eight different reference guides on the subject, because I couldn't find one that was very useful. Not only did I find it difficult and time-consuming to search for answers to my questions in these manuals, but even when I succeeded in finding the information I was looking for, the instructions usually proved to be confusing.

Given that the majority of computer users do their word processing with Microsoft Word, it was difficult to understand why no one had thought to create a truly useful reference guide on the subject, i.e., something resembling a dictionary or thesaurus wherein the user could look up answers in alphabetical order. Since I could find nothing remotely close to this concept in bookstores, I decided that the only way I was going to have such a resource at my disposal was to create it myself.

Through a combination of lessons, studying, and endless hours of trial and error, I became what could loosely be referred to as a "Word expert." As time passed, I began sharing my homemade reference guide with friends and business associates, and their enthusiastic comments were quite surprising. In fact, many of them urged me to expand my customized "book" and make it available to the general public. I finally decided to take them up on their suggestion, because, based on my own experience, I was convinced that the concept I had created could be of great value to Microsoft Word users.

The project involved about a year and a half of detailed, exhausting work, which was about a year longer than I had anticipated it would take. My problem was that I became maniacally obsessed with making the reference guide perfect, and the result was a 656-page book I dubbed the *Wordasaurus Quick-Answer Guide*. My concept was much like learning a foreign language while living in another country; i.e., a user could become adept at Word while doing his normal, day-to-day work.

Except for one problem: I had vastly underestimated the impact of how quickly Microsoft upgraded its software (on average, every eighteen to twenty-four months). The *Wordasaurus Quick-Answer Guide* was based on Microsoft Word 95, which most people were using when I started the project. But by the time my book came off the press, most users had moved on to Word 97, and, worse, Microsoft was beginning to talk about Word 2000. After two years of hard labor, I was facing the prospect of two more years to create a book on Word 2000—just in time for Microsoft to release Word XP (2002). Not being attracted to masochism, I decided to pass.

My painful experience was a grim reminder of what an important factor urgency is in the marketplace, regardless of how much value one creates. The problem is that value is perishable. It's a grave mistake to fall so in love with a project that it prevents you from getting it done in a timely fashion. The best laid plans of mice and men are sometimes dead on arrival. True, I had taken action by undertaking the project and sticking with it day in and day out, but because I had gone to a perfection extreme probably ten times beyond what was necessary to outdistance the competition, I forfeited the opportunity to take *marketing* action. And when it comes to a product's success, marketing is, without question, *the* most critical action of all. It was a classic case of perfection being an enemy of good.

Also, because your mind's primary focus can be on only one thing at a time, to the degree you focus on perfection, you aren't able to focus on substance. In other words, perfection tends to focus on details (form) rather than the real objective (substance) of a project. I had the substance of my reference guide completed in six months, and, in retrospect, I probably didn't increase the value to the end user by more than 5 to 10 percent by polishing it for another year.

FREEDOM FROM "*WHAT IF?*"

The essence of the *What if?* problem can be seen in the saving of too many documents and files. Saving mountains of paper is a result of the subconscious mind's annoying habit of asking, "What if?" "This file contains documents that I haven't looked at in five years, but I don't feel comfortable throwing it away. What *if* I need to refer to some of the documents at a later date?"

"Please, Mr. Gates, don't turn me away. I'll even agree to testify on your behalf before the Justice Department."

The *What if?* compulsion is part of a broader compulsion known as the CYA (Cover Your Anatomy) philosophy. This is a philosophy that places an inordinately high priority on trying to make certain that you will never be blamed for anything and will always be able to quickly find the precise item or answer you need to solve any problem in your life. Living a CYA life is a huge obstacle to taking action.

In addition, it tends to result in a person's garage being filled with cartons of twenty-year-old files, a suffocating enslavement to which I can attest. I didn't begin making a serious dent in getting rid of old junk files until I started asking myself, "What are the consequences of not having this file or document if I should need it down the road?" In all but a few cases, the answer was that not only were the odds overwhelmingly against my ever needing the file or document, but clearly my world would not come to an end if I did need it and couldn't put my hands on it.

Another example of a CYA life is to be found in the compulsion to fill out and mail warranty cards. Have you ever purchased an extensive computer setup with a variety of software and add-ons? After the technician finishes setting you up, he leaves behind empty boxes and a stack of warranty cards. Filling out warranty cards gives me chest pains. Which would be bad enough in itself, but what makes it all the more painful is that you know you probably will never need to use the warranties. The few times I have called upon a manufacturer to make good on a warranty, either the warranty had already expired or the repairs could be done without the warranty card being on file.

Basing your life on the question *What if?* is a compulsion that can enslave you till the day you die. *What if?* is not real; it's hypothetical. Better to spend your limited amount of time and energy resources on what *is,* and take bold action accordingly.

FREEDOM FROM THE NEED TO PROVE YOU'RE RIGHT

An obsessive need to prove you're right gets in the way of taking the kind of action that can move you closer to achieving your goals. A classic example of this is a painful experience I endured many years ago, when I was much younger and much more ignorant. My wife had noticed some damage to our roof, and made an appointment with a roofing company ("Stick-it-to-'em Roofing") to come out and fix it. More than an hour after the scheduled time, the roofers still had not arrived, and I was on the verge of being late for an appointment.

Just as I was preparing to leave the house, the doorbell rang. Sure enough, standing before me were two men from Stick-it-to-'em Roofing. They could barely speak English, and what words they did manage to utter were camouflaged by a thick Spanish accent. Realizing they would probably have trouble understanding me, I spoke slowly and clearly, explaining that I was about to leave the house. Then, as an afterthought, I said, "Look, if you don't need me here, you can go up and fix the roof, but I have to leave in two minutes. The two men nodded pleasantly, and uttered some more "Spanglish" that indicated they would go ahead and do the repairs.

A couple of minutes later, I got into my car, started the engine, and began to back out of the garage. Suddenly, I heard a loud commotion and something hitting the back of my car. For a second, I thought it might be an earthquake. I jumped out and went around to the rear of the car to see what had happened. To my surprise, a long, heavy ladder was lying on the right rear of my car. Then, from the roof, I heard familiar voices excitedly yelling at me in apologetic Spanglish. I was quite disturbed, and angrily asked the men why they had put their ladder behind my car, especially since I had just told them I was leaving. It goes without saying that I could not understand their response, but they continued to address me in apologetic tones.

As they shimmied their way to the ground, I examined the right side and trunk of my car, and was dismayed to see that the damage from the ladder was extensive. I told the two workers that Stick-it-to-'em Roofing was going to have to pay for the damages, in response to which they kept repeating, with apologetic gestures, "Sí! Sí!" I assumed that Stick-it-to-'em Roofing would be embarrassed over their employees' ignorant placement of the ladder, and the main focus of my thoughts was on wondering how long I would have to be without my car while the necessary repairs were being made.

Over the next week, I placed about a dozen phone calls to Stick-it-to-'em Roofing, continually being referred from one person to another, until I was finally assured that I was talking to the individual who handled the company's customer complaints ("Mr. Cute"). Mr. Cute claimed to know nothing about the incident, but said he would check it out and get back to me in a few days. After a week passed without a call, I started calling Mr. Cute every day and left a half-dozen messages for him without receiving a single return call.

"You imbeciles! Stick-it-to-'em Roofing is going to have to pay for this."

About the time I was on the verge of losing patience with being ignored, Mr. Cute (not knowing that it was me calling) finally picked up the receiver on one of my calls. He told me that Stick-it-to-'em's insurance company handled all claims, and that I should have my insurance company call them. Irritated, I said, "Look, just pay for the damage you did to my car, and if you want to collect from your insurance company, that's your business." Mr. Cute said he would have to check it out with Mr. Stickitoem himself and would get back to me.

Weeks later, when I finally succeeded in getting Mr. Cute on the phone again, he explained that there was nothing more he could do about the matter, because—surprise, surprise—the workers who had come to my house were now supposedly claiming they had told me that they were going to put the ladder behind my car, and that it was therefore *my* fault. I was livid. Quite obviously, the workers' new story was contrived by the company, and I would have to be pretty naïve not to assume that they would be willing to swear to whatever the company instructed them to say.

"First," I said, "these guys can't speak English, so even if they had told me they were going to put their ladder behind my garage door, I would not have understood them. Second, nobody in his right mind would tell someone that he's going to put a ladder directly behind that person's garage door when he has the entire house to use. Third, I don't for a second believe they actually told you that. What I do believe is that *you* told them to say it. Fourth, why didn't you tell me all this months ago when I first spoke to you, instead of implying that who was at fault was not even an issue?" I went on to tell Mr. Cute that unless Stick-it-to-'em Roofing paid for the damage to my car within a week, I would file suit in small claims court. Danger signal: My emotions were now in total control.

Needless to say, no one from the company called me again, let alone paid for the damage, so, as promised, I filed suit in small claims court. Over the next several months, I stood in lines at the courthouse, burned the midnight oil filling out legal forms, visited car-repair shops and secured estimates, did a mountain of research, and spent obscene amounts of time standing over a copying machine and making copies of pertinent documents, sorting papers, and setting up files for the case. To a fly on the wall, it must have appeared as though I were preparing for a murder trial. Lots of action, to be sure—but it was *stupid* action.

What, in fact, had happened was that I had inadvertently developed an obsession to prove I was right over an issue not worthy of my time. As Stick-it-to-'em Roofing injected one obstacle after another into this penny-ante case in an effort to stall, I finally started coming to my senses. I realized that I had allowed my emotions to entrap me in a no-win situation. There was no doubt in my mind that the court would order Stick-it-to-'em Roofing to pay me $2,000 in damages, but that wouldn't even begin to make a dent in the income I had lost as a result of my vigorous pursuit of justice. Worse, the stress and anxiety I had suffered from this distasteful mess were impossible to quantify.

When the court date finally arrived, I showed up at 8:00 A.M., eager to bring the matter to a conclusion. There is nothing quite as stimulating as sitting on a hard wooden bench in a courthouse and listening to small claims cases—"Mr. Smith's dog ruined my rose garden"; "Mr. Wilson wrote our store a personal check for his groceries, ate the evidence, then claimed the food was spoiled and stopped payment on his check"; "Mrs. O'Neil's son drove his car over my lawn"; etc., etc., etc. As the hours droned on, I didn't know whether to laugh, cry, or yawn.

Finally, the moment of truth—my case was called. A shyster-looking attorney ("Legalsleaze") in a vomit-colored polyester suit came forward on behalf of Stick-it-to-'em Roofing. As I stood dutifully next to him before the presiding judge, the first thing that crossed my mind was that Stick-it-to-'em Roofing had probably bartered his fees. Why else would Legalsleaze use the same stuff on his hair that the company used for tarring roofs?

The judge then asked Legalsleaze to state his position on the case. What came out of his mouth was yet another reminder of how the legal system works—which is to say that it doesn't. Without a trace of a smirk, he said that since his client believed I was at fault, it wanted to sue *me* to recover its legal fees, and that would entail "full discovery"—meaning depositions, interrogatories, and more. All this would require at least a year to accomplish, perhaps two years if enough clever stalling tactics were employed, and Legals-leaze began moving in that direction by requesting that the case be moved to Superior Court for a full-blown trial. Still reeling, I listened as the judge said that he had no choice but to grant Legals-leaze his request.

As I left the courthouse, I laughed out loud at my naïveté. The next day, I dropped the suit, licked my wounds, and got back to working on constructive matters. I had been action personified in pursuit of justice, but the problem was that my actions were based on emotion. It was a painful, time-wasting experience that served as a grim reminder of how important it is to be vigilant about not becoming obsessed with proving you're right.

The best way I know to become free of the self-imposed enslave-ment to prove you're right is to ask yourself if the resolution of a point of contention is really all that important in the overall scheme of things. Two thousand dollars may have seemed like a significant sum of money when I began my Stick-it-to-'em legal journey, but by the time I came to my senses and threw in the towel, it was a pittance compared to the hours I had wasted and the stress I had endured. It was a great reminder of how irrational it is to spend signi-ficant amounts of time (not to mention mental energy and financial resources) trying to rectify a wrong that involves a relatively small amount of money.

Fortunately, the Stick-it-to-'em Roofing episode was an excep-tion for me. A day rarely goes by without my hearing people say many things with which I disagree, but I rarely argue with them. In fact, the more confident I am that I'm right, the less inclined I am to challenge an incorrect statement. I feel that if I know I'm right, I have nothing to gain by telling someone he's wrong. It could cause hard feelings or, worse, it could lead to a debate, and I've already covered the dangers of getting sidetracked by debates in Chapter 5.

An exception to this is when it's an individual who is involved in a project that I'm working on, and he makes an incorrect statement that is material to the success of the project. In such a case, there obviously is a necessity for the other person to understand the facts. Another exception is when I'm *not* 100 percent certain that I'm right, in which case it is, of course, prudent to discuss the matter with the other person.

I should also point out that in both business and personal matters, the cost of proving you're right often can be too high in terms of creating bad will. This is especially true if the person you're trying to prove wrong is a customer, supervisor, boss, or even a friend. The instant gratification of flaunting the fact that you were right can prove to be fatal in the long term. At a minimum, the cost of proving you're right tends to turn off even people who are normally supportive of you. What good is being right if it puts a negative stamp on you?

FREEDOM FROM "WHY?"

After decades of observing super-successful people, I have come to the conclusion that a significant percentage of them tend to be shallow thinkers. Consider:

- When Steven Spielberg was a guest on *Larry King Live*, King asked him if he ever thought about what it was that allowed him to come up with one creative project after another. With a perplexed expression on his face, he answered, "Gee, I've never really thought about it. I think I'd be afraid that if I thought about it too much, I might lose whatever it is that makes it possible for me to do it."

- When, in one of Mark McGwire's many interviews after breaking Roger Maris's home-run record, he was asked how he had managed to handle the pressure, he replied, "I don't know how I did it. I don't know if I want to know how I did it." (I know, I know—illegal substances—but, still, seventy home runs is seventy home runs.)

- When Frank Sinatra died, newspapers around the world covered his life and death in minute detail. Of particular interest to me was an article that listed some of "Sinatra's Rules." One of the more fascinating things he was purported to have believed was that "people shouldn't think too much."

I realize that some readers might find my observation about successful people to be insulting, but that all depends on their premise. If someone believes that deep thinking is inherently good, then I suppose a lack of deep thinking could be construed as bad. But if deep thinking is not viewed as either good or bad, it becomes just a matter of fascination; i.e., why do some people think deeply and others don't?

Even more important is to examine the ramifications of being a deep thinker and the ramifications of not being a deep thinker. If Frank Sinatra and, say, a legendary writer/philosopher like Fyodor Dostoevsky had each been asked to look at a rock and then relate their thoughts about what they had seen, their answers undoubtedly would have been quite different. From what we know about each of these men, it would be reasonable to assume that Sinatra might have said something like, "I see a rock. What's the big deal?" By contrast, Dostoevsky might have said something like, "I see a rock, but I wonder what is inside the rock and what it's made of? Why does the rock exist, and what is its true purpose?"

Thus, Sinatra would have dispensed with the rock question in seconds, while Dostoevsky probably would have added it to a storehouse of similar questions that consumed his mind, to be thought about periodically throughout his life. Which one is better off depends on your premise. If fame, fortune, and fun are your objectives, then Sinatra would be your role model. If intellectually dismantling everything that crosses your path gives you pleasure, then Dostoevsky would be your man.

As always, I lean toward moderation. If you're serious about searching for truth, you are compelled to do a considerable amount of deep thinking and reflection. Like most things in life, however, deep thinking becomes a problem when carried to the extreme of evolving into what I call the *Why?* Syndrome. Unless you're working toward a master's degree in rocks, is it really important to know *why* a rock exists? From a utilitarian point of view, the fact that a rock exists and that you have no use for it is sufficient information. The simplicity of such an observation allows the utilitarian to move quickly on to more important matters in his life, which is much more conducive to success.

"Hmmm . . . I see a rock. But why does the rock exist, and how do I know that the inside of the rock does not consist of rice pudding?"

Obsessive *Why?* thinkers probably tend to have more stress, higher blood pressure, and far less productivity than non-*Why?* thinkers. To the extent you suffer from any of these maladies, you may want to take a more vigorous approach to freeing yourself from many of the *Why?*'s in your life. Perhaps the most unsettling thing about being a *Why?* thinker is that when he exits this life, he may not know a whole lot more about it than someone who has never thought to ask why

149

about anything. Actually, there's one thing even worse: What if you *do* end up knowing more about life than people who never ask why, but in the end you discover that it doesn't matter?

For example, if spirituality is a high priority with you when it comes to a search for truth, consider the possibility that "connecting" with a Divine Power may be more difficult for the individual whose mind is cluttered by a million and one *Why?*s. There has been speculation in some psychology quarters that a mentally retarded person, because his mind is uncluttered, may actually possess a superior capacity to be spiritual.

I am not in any way suggesting that you should curb your search for truth. The search for truth is an essential ingredient for success that must be the primary guide for your actions. What I am suggesting, however, is that you should be selective when it comes to asking the question *Why?*, because it has the potential to become another one of those incredibly powerful action stoppers. It would be an oxymoron to say that a person leads a *Why?*-oriented, action-oriented life.

FREEDOM FROM GROUPING

Give the major television networks credit for one thing, they understand that sexual decadence and racial hatred sell. By featuring these sick themes ad nauseam on talk shows, they succeed in titillating their audiences into wanting still more.

My memory takes me back to one of the more absurd offerings on one of these tired subjects, which was aired in the early 1990s by Phil Donahue, one-time king of talk-show decadence. On this particular episode, Donahue's guests included three young black activists and a black Princeton University professor with a 1960s activist background. With Donahue demonically pouring verbal gasoline on the racial fires, the black activists let the whites in the audience know, in no uncertain terms, that they considered them to be the enemy.

One groveling young white man in the audience explained that he was a member of an all-white acting company, and that his group was in the process of producing a show about civil rights. With a whimpering plea in his voice, he asked the black activists, "Am I the enemy, too?" To which one of the activists responded inexplicably, "Do you love America?" The white actor meekly answered in the affirmative. The activist, smelling blood, admonished him with, "Well, you got problems." Blacks in the audience hooted and howled their approval; whites in the audience booed.

Another activist went into a long tirade about whites owing him a debt for enslaving his ancestors, defiantly warning, "And we're here to collect it!" Blacks in the audience hooted and howled their approval; whites in the audience booed.

During an unintelligible diatribe, one of the activists suddenly yelled out, again for no explicable reason, "I'm an African! I'm in exile!" Nice rhetoric, but few blacks are seriously interested in leaving the United States, where most would agree they are far better off than blacks in any African country. Walter Williams, a black economics professor at George Mason University and a champion of self-responsibility, put it succinctly when he asked, "What has Afrocentrism done for Africa?"

Most black Americans realize that white folks are never going to embrace blacks who cling to so-called Afrocentrism. The more some blacks choose to group themselves as "African Americans," the more the fires of racism will be stoked. The biggest obstacles to diffusing this idiotic, out-of-touch attitude are the black hate-mongers who ludicrously insist that every black person who makes it in America has sold out. Who can forget the nauseating remarks of a pathetic and aging (demented?) Harry Belafonte, who, on national television, referred to Secretary of State Colin Powell as a "house slave" in the Bush administration?

Self-anointed black leaders, desperate to continue perpetuating the grouping of blacks, so fear people of color who espouse self-responsibility that they will do almost anything to undermine their message. Those who have ignored their hate messages and taken action to better their lives have become business leaders, doctors, talk-show hosts, news commentators, engineers, and professionals of all kinds. Such success is anathema to old-school black "leaders" like Jesse Jackson and Al Sharpton who feel threatened by individuals who act on their own.

Now CONTRAST THE DONAHUE episode to an interesting conversation I had shortly after I took control of the health products company in New Zealand that I wrote about earlier. I had persuaded a young black lady from North America ("Marilyn") to move Down Under and assume the position of Operations Director. She was a very serious, self-confident, efficient individual who had a low threshold for nonsense. During one of our many conversations about life in New Zealand versus life in America, the question of racism came up. Both of us were impressed with how comfortable New Zealand was with the integration of its British conquerors and the native Maori people.

Inevitably, the conversation turned to race relations in America and the question of political correctness in addressing black Americans. When I mentioned the term *African American*, Marilyn grimaced and said, "I cringe when people refer to me as an African American. I wasn't born in Africa, I don't know anything about Africa, I've never been to Africa, and I don't plan on ever going to Africa. So how do I qualify as an African American?" Good question. What Marilyn was expressing was a desire to not have her identity buried in a group, particularly a group she knew little about. Individualistic action and the desire or need to be thought of in a collective way are mutually exclusive objectives.

To be sure, valid generalizations can be made about people based on sex, nationality, race, and, yes, even religious beliefs. For example, if you stated a self-evident truth such as American blacks, on average, tend to become professional athletes more often than do American whites, you certainly would be right. You also would be statistically correct if you stated that American blacks, on average, tend to commit more violent crimes than do American whites. If you stated that Jews, on average, tend to become professional athletes less often than non-Jews, your statement would be beyond dispute. You also would be correct if you stated that Jews, on average, tend to commit fewer violent crimes than non-Jews.

Because such generalizations are supported by hard facts, they are perfectly valid, notwithstanding the ugly shadow of political correctness. But let's look at these four examples from a more relevant slant. Approximately 99.99 percent of American blacks are *not* professional athletes, and the vast majority of the American black population has never been found guilty of committing a violent crime.

What about Jews in professional sports? Many people believe that Sandy Koufax was the greatest pitcher in major league baseball history; Dolph Schayes is considered to be one of the fifty greatest National Basketball Association players of all time; and Sid Gilman, an all-American himself in college, was considered by his peers to be one of the greatest coaching strategists in the NFL for decades. So, even though the percentage of Jews in professional sports is low, a number of Jewish *individuals* managed to become superstars.

Jewish criminals? How would you like to wake up one morning and find Meyer Lansky, Bugsy Siegel, or Mickey Cohen on your doorstep? These *individuals* operated outside the accurate *generalizations* about Jews and violent crime.

The point is that people can make true generalizations about groups to their heart's content, but such generalizations have no bearing on you, the *individual*. The more you glorify such factors as sex, race, nationality, and religion, the more you submit to a subtle form of enslavement. Taking action is about individuals, not groups. Instead of fretting over what people say about "your group," use your energy to focus on *your* specific and unique talents. If you want the playing field to be leveled, do it by taking action that creates value, not through group action (which is but a euphemism for *group force*).

Be ever vigilant about not becoming prey to any of the thousands of moral hucksters, tyrants, charlatans, and political activists who have anointed themselves leaders of one group or another. Acting on their rhetoric to throw in your lot with a group is a drastic move away from individualism. It is the individualist who stands the best chance of achieving long-term happiness and success, because individualism promotes action. And it is action on the part of individuals that breaks the stereotype molds for women, blacks, Jews, gays, Mexican Americans, Arab Americans, the physically handicapped, the elderly, and every other group ever conceived of by con artists whose livelihoods depend upon their ability to promote group action.

The next time one of these unemployed power-mongers organizes a protest march to demand special rights (under the guise of equal rights) for some group that presumptuously claims you as a member, do yourself a favor: Stay home and read a good book on individualism. That's an action that will produce both short- and long-term benefits.

FREEDOM FROM HATRED

Racial hatred is not the only kind of hatred in the world, but it does serve as an extreme example of just how senseless, irrational, and self-destructive hatred can be. Unfortunately, the efforts of well-meaning people who counter this emotion by espousing love are, for the most part, misplaced. After thousands of years of urging people throughout the world to let go of their hatred, there is more animosity and loathing today than ever before. Urging people to "stop the hating" has about as much effect as urging people to buy your product without telling them why it is in their best interest to do so. You cannot force someone to love another person. As history has repeatedly demonstrated, whenever force has been used to quell hatred, the hatred has rebounded many times over.

If you told me that you hated someone, and you asked for my advice on the matter, I would appeal to your self-interest. I probably would submit a list of reasons why it is not in *your* best interest to continue hating the individual in question. My list would include such things as:

1. Hatred is a negative emotion that breeds negative thoughts, and negative thoughts produce negative results. Among other things, your thoughts attract other negative people, who, in turn, stir up your hatred even more. Elevated levels of hatred can drain you of emotional energy, poison your body, and paralyze your spirit.

2. Hating is an extremely painful mental activity, and since the mind can focus on only one thing at a time, any time wasted on hating impedes your efforts to take constructive action.

3. Ask yourself what the endgame of your hatred is. If there is no endgame—i.e., no purpose—what's the point? If your

objective is simply to hate, then it becomes the height of irrationality, because your hatred is based on emotion rather than reason. Why use up valuable time and energy resources to engage in a negative activity that has no definable purpose? Other than cases where people are prepared to use violence against those they hate, hate is usually an end in itself.

4. If your hatred for someone is based on something he did to you, the more time and energy you spend on hating that person, the more you allow him to hurt you. There is much truth to the motto that living well is the best revenge. Convert hatred into motivation to succeed, and let your success be a blanket response to everyone you dislike. The more success you experience, the less time you have for petty matters such as hating.

Put another way, you don't have to love your enemies; just don't give them the satisfaction of hating them. If I were going to create the perfect human being, I would make one of his chief attributes the ability to instantly strike from his mind all thoughts of his enemies—including and especially all hateful thoughts—not just because such an attribute would be virtuous, but because, from a pragmatic standpoint, it would free his mind to work on more constructive pursuits.

FREEDOM FROM GUILT

It is conventional wisdom that guilt is an unwarranted state of mind, which means there is never a valid reason for feeling guilty. But is this wisdom really sound? Guilt, according to one dictionary, is a feeling of responsibility or remorse for some offense, crime, or wrong, whether real or imagined. So there are two questions to address regarding guilt: First, who should define what constitutes *wrong*? Second, assuming the first question can be answered, are you actually guilty of the alleged wrongdoing?

WHO SHOULD DEFINE WHAT CONSTITUTES WRONG?
Unfortunately, a great deal of guilt is induced by the opinions and moral beliefs of others. There will never be a shortage of people who

are more than happy to admonish you for doing something wrong. It's your job to make conscious, rational decisions for yourself, so never relinquish that task to others—especially strangers. When it comes to morality, in particular, you must put into place, and live by, a code of ethics with which you feel comfortable. Who among us has the knowledge or wisdom to lay down moral guidelines for others? It is the character of *your* soul that should determine right and wrong for *you,* so long as your version of right does not include the use of force or fraud against anyone else. Let the other person's code of ethics be the guide for *his* actions.

ARE YOU GUILTY OF WRONGDOING?

If, based on your knowledge of the facts and your personal code of ethics, you conclude that you have committed a wrong, then honesty and integrity compel you to face up to that fact and, to the extent possible, make reparations to the appropriate party. At a minimum, an unequivocal apology is in order, which is an action that almost always engenders respect. Guilt, then, is a good thing to the extent you have a sound reason for feeling guilty, and provided it motivates you to take positive action.

By the same token, when an individual with a sound moral infrastructure is not guilty of wrongdoing, it just as important for him to refuse to be burdened by guilt as it is for him to apologize and make amends when he is guilty. To decide whether or not guilt is called for in any given situation, be sure to check the basic premises of anyone who admonishes you for your actions. Unfortunately, most people, especially people with high public profiles, are easily intimidated when activist groups accuse them of violating the tenets of some cause or agenda they are promoting.

For many years now, the so-called sweatshop issue has been among the most chic of these causes. I vividly recall, back in 1996, what happened when Kathie Lee Gifford was loudly criticized by union-supported, anti-sweatshop activists. Because she lacked either courage or knowledge—or both—she cried on national television, renounced the error of her ways for allowing her clothing line to be produced in low-wage factories in Honduras, and assured her public that she would have it stopped immediately.

It sounded eerily like Chinese capitalists who confessed their fabricated sins and were sent to rehabilitation camps in the heyday of Red China's purges. Instead of checking the premises of her detractors and announcing that she was *proud* to be responsible for creating employment for thousands of workers in an impoverished third-world country, Gifford allowed clueless, left-wing child activists to intimidate her into feeling guilty and confessing her so-called sins on national television.

Kathie Lee Gifford's unfounded guilt feelings not only harmed her financially, but, worse, resulted in thousands of poor people in Honduras suddenly finding themselves unemployed. It was a classic example of the historical problem of guilt bringing wealth-creating action to a screeching halt. Unfounded guilt is always a barrier to action and an arch nemesis of progress.

Unless you accumulate your wealth by defrauding little old ladies out of their life savings, never feel guilty for being financially successful. Working hard in an effort to get ahead in life is a noble activity, so long as you do not commit aggression against others. On the contrary, you should feel proud that you are a net producer for society rather than a net consumer. Achieving success stems from creating value for others, so if you genuinely want to make the world a better place for everyone, keep your focus on achieving your goals— *and don't feel guilty about it.*

FREEDOM FROM ENVY

Pretty much everything I said about hate is true for envy as well. Envy goes hand in hand with the loser's syndrome of transforming desires into rights, because misplaced desire often stems from envy. I should point out that there is a subtle difference between the terms *jealousy* and *envy*. Jealousy denotes a feeling of resentment toward someone who has gained or achieved something that one feels he instead deserves. Envy denotes a longing to *possess* something that someone else owns or has achieved.

Envy is the more perverse of these two negative emotions, because it has nothing to do with success or failure. If someone thinks he deserves the promotion you received, he may be jealous of you. But if he covets your new Mercedes because he's discontented with his ten-year-old Chevy, it would be wise not to leave your keys in the ignition at night, because you have an envious person hot on your trail.

At its extreme, envy becomes an obsession to destroy those who are more fortunate than the envious individual, an obsession that has fueled repeated social revolutions through the centuries, the most famous of which was the 1917 Bolshevik Revolution in Russia. The envious masses in that somber country, led by power-hungry tyrants, took action, but their negative (envious) actions led them into slavery for seventy years. The quality of their lives didn't improve until Perestroika began to free them in 1986 and gave them the opportunity to take action to better their own existence.

Envy-based discontent is so intense that it allows the envious to justify virtually any action, no matter how heinous it may be. Vladimir Lenin, leader of the Bolshevik Revolution, made no bones about this when he boasted, "To tell the truth is a petty bourgeois habit, whereas for us to lie is justified by our objectives."

In the event you have a trace of envy in your soul, it is much to your advantage to consciously try to free yourself from this action-stifling emotional disease. Being envious of others is a huge time-waster that an individual serious about improving his lot in life cannot afford, and the best way to eradicate this mental menace is to understand how wealth is achieved through the creation of value.

Those who are the most envious are people who have not discovered this truth, or, on having discovered it, are not willing to compete with others by creating value in the marketplace. A down-with-the-rich mentality, bolstered by a zero-sum view of wealth (i.e., where one person's gain is another person's loss), is an immature, even childish, view of the world. Nonetheless, this envy-based doctrine is continually being reinforced by politicians and university professors worldwide, particularly those who teach economics.

Every age has its so-called robber barons—from J. P. Morgan to Howard Hughes to Michael Milken to Bill Gates. Being the richest man in the world made Gates an easy target for the envious. The reality, of course, is that Gates became the world's richest man because he has probably created more value for more people—particularly people of lesser means—than any human being in history. The measly billions he personally accumulated pale by comparison to the uncountable trillions of dollars people have earned, and will continue to earn, as a result of his entrepreneurial exploits.

Bill Gates and Microsoft dramatically changed the world for the better, improving the lives of even those people who don't know how to use a computer. Even so, Gates, like his buddy Warren Buffett, caved in to the shouts of the envy crowd, allowed his guilt feelings and left-wing wife to overwhelm his intellect, and made the decision to spend his life helping poor people in Third World countries. While his intentions may be noble, and I applaud his efforts, the reality is that his charitable work will never come close to helping as many people improve their lives as did his exploits at the helm of Microsoft.

The zero-sum-wealth perception is ignorance at its worst. The reality, of course, is that wealth creation is limitless. In the simplest of terms, if you make $1 billion this year and my income is zero, these two facts are totally unrelated. Further, and luckily for me, your making $1 billion does not affect my opportunity to earn as much as I possibly can in the marketplace. I am not limited by what *you* earn, but by my own ability and willingness to take action and work hard to create wealth. What an exciting and awesome reality.

Freedom from envy is a freedom that requires vigilance, because vote-hungry politicians and envious, disgruntled people all around us are constantly sprinkling our brains with envy's poisonous seeds. Whenever you sense you are a target of this emotional poison, simply ignore the words of those who throw mental darts at you, thank them for their good intentions, then tell them that you won't be needing their services anymore.

FREEDOM FROM PEER PRESSURE

The desire to impress others is one of the worst forms of mental imprisonment. It not only requires a great deal of time and energy, but it eats away at a person's self-esteem as well. There is nothing more degrading than knowing, whether or not it is consciously acknowledged, that one is saying something, doing something, or buying something with the primary purpose of impressing others. What could be more at odds with taking rational action than basing your actions on what you believe will please others?

Unfortunately, to one extent or another, everyone says and does things that are motivated by peer pressure. Even the most forthright among us are "on stage" from time to time, whether or not we are consciously aware of it. As with everything in life, however, in excess such performing can be very harmful—even fatal.

Peer pressure becomes visible in grade school, though it actually begins much earlier in life. It is a phenomenon that eats away at the personalities of children year after year, all too often resulting in lost souls. Worse, millions of children have become fatalities—through such activities as drug abuse, drunk driving, and gang fights—as a result of yielding to peer pressure.

Those who are lucky enough to survive elementary, middle, and high school usually begin the long road back to freedom from peer pressure in their mid to late twenties. Some are fortunate enough to travel this freedom road rather quickly, others more slowly, and still others hardly at all. The longer it takes to achieve a reasonable degree of freedom from peer pressure, the longer a person experiences the internal humiliation of feeling like a grade-school child trying to impress his classmates.

This degrading human trait cuts across economic barriers. Inner-city gang members strive for conformity and acceptance—expressed through violent behavior—as much or more than do suburban, midlevel executives vying for membership in the right country club. Indeed, eliminate the phenomenon of peer pressure, and our prisons would probably be half empty.

Ultimately, peer pressure evolves into self-pressure, i.e., motivation from within to impress others. In suburbia, it spawns affectation—the effort to make others believe that one possesses wealth or qualities he does not really possess. People who suffer from affectation to an extreme have lost their identities. They are, in fact, the most imprisoned people on earth. While they feign dignity, it is a trait that, in reality, they totally lack. Affectation stems from an immature desire to "keep up with the Joneses," and having lived in the suburbs of many cities throughout the world, I can assure you that this desire is systemic in the human race.

Affectation almost always metastasizes into an unhealthy attachment to material belongings, which becomes yet another form of self-imprisonment. Buddha warned of this imprisonment when he observed that, "All unhappiness is caused by attachment." I like material possessions as much as anyone, but I am no longer obsessed by them as I was when I was much younger. Obsessive attachment to material possessions is almost certain to lead to unhappiness, because it gets in the way of concentrating on a worthwhile purpose in life.

Focusing on money, in fact, can actually retard the desire to take meaningful action. Viktor Frankl referred to this "will to money" as a "paradoxical intention," contending that the more we make something a target, the more likely we are to miss it. I find it interesting that so many of the world's wealthiest individuals seem, at least on the surface, not to be motivated by material possessions.

Conformity is nothing more than a method for achieving acceptance. But the more a person focuses on gaining acceptance and popularity, the less he is able to focus on taking action to develop the very qualities that bring acceptance and popularity as natural consequences—such as strengthening his personal infrastructure and creating value for others.

FREEDOM TO FOCUS ON LIFE

The response to the constraints of day-to-day life is often a little voice inside one's head that shouts, "Leave me alone!" This is why most of us relate so well to the theme song from the Broadway musical *Man of La Mancha*. It does a marvelous job of glorifying the elusive concept known as *freedom*. Don Quixote's words—"*I've got to be me . . . I've got to be free . . . I want to live, not merely survive*"—are enough to make one fantasize about quitting his job, leaving his possessions behind, and boarding a plane headed for some faraway paradise in the Mediterranean or South Pacific. Or, less exotically, simply turning left at Oak Street one day instead of right, as in Roy Clark's thought-provoking song "Right or Left at Oak Street."

However, rather than opting for such a dramatic approach to achieving freedom, a much more sensible alternative is to stay right where you are, work hard at freeing yourself from non-constructive pursuits and obstacles, such as those I've discussed in this chapter, and focus instead on a life of action. The wonderful truth of the matter is that there's a whole lot more to life than merely surviving.

CHAPTER 7

Self-Disciplined Action

The best discipline, maybe the only discipline that really works, is self-discipline.
— WALTER KIECHEL III

HAVE YOU EVER THOUGHT about how many action choices you make in a day's time? Twenty-five? Fifty? One hundred? Not even close. In reality, you make more choices every day of your life than you can count. When your alarm or clock radio goes off each morning, you choose whether to jump out of bed or pull the covers over your head. If you opt for the latter, every second you remain in bed represents a choice you are making, so if you lie in bed for one minute, you're actually making the choice to stay in bed at least sixty times (using seconds as a measuring stick).

This decision-making process continues as you go through the ritual of getting up and out of the house. To shave or not to shave? To shower or not to shower? Which clothes to wear? What to eat for breakfast? Whether or not to watch the morning news? Whether to move fast or slowly?

As you can see, most of these choices are not of great importance. But others, such as decisions about love relationships, changing careers, or making an investment, can have a dramatic effect on your life. That's why it's so important to apply self-discipline to your actions. To the extent one's actions are based on emotion and impulse rather than intellect and rationality, they are likely to lead to bad consequences. When you allow your emotions to rule, you subject yourself to emotional enslavement, and never is a person less free than when he is enslaved by his emotions.

Regardless of the degree of importance, the fact of the matter is that everything you do throughout the day is based on choice. Many of your choices are made unconsciously, while others may require intense concentration over a long period of time. To the extent you put yourself on autopilot and allow too many of those choices to be made unconsciously, you invite bad consequences into your life. By making conscious, rational choices, you dramatically increase your chances of achieving long-term success.

When I say that many choices in our everyday lives are made unconsciously, I mean that we don't make a *conscious effort* to make rational decisions, which, in turn, means that we act on impulse much of the time. Curiosity may have killed the cat, but I would remind you that impulsive action killed him as well. I know that to be a fact, because I've seen him lying motionless on the road, paying the price for having bolted in front of an oncoming vehicle. Cats act on impulse. Good news: You're not a cat. You have an intellect, and, contrary to what reality-TV producers would like you to believe, it is not against the law to use it. It's simply not a great idea for a human being to base too many of his actions on impulse.

Not long ago, while driving at a relatively high rate of speed on a well-traveled road, I spotted three young boys standing on the raised median strip, waiting to cross. Two of the boys darted across the busy street, having made the impulsive judgment that they could get to the other side before my car hit them. The third boy lunged forward slightly, then pulled back. If I could, I would have stopped my car, given him a high five, and said, "Good choice, young man." Immediately after I passed the boys, the thought occurred to me that the odds of living a long, successful life were much better for the boy who demonstrated self-control by not bolting in front of my car than for his two impulsive friends.

We're always hopeful that our children will be the ones to have the good sense not to go along with the crowd and engage in impulsive, dangerous actions, because, as millions of people have discovered through first-hand experience, a single impulsive action can be fatal. Which is why so many parents say things like "Make good choices" to their children when they go out with friends. Bad choices have led to the death of millions of young people—particularly teenagers— over the span of recorded history.

Having the self-discipline to make sound choices is an important factor in the success equation. By *sound choices*, I'm talking about rational decisions that are more likely to bring success over the long term as opposed to decisions focused on producing instant gratific- ation. Self-discipline, then, is about restraining, or regulating, one's actions, i.e., repressing the instinct to act impulsively in favor of taking rational actions that are long-term oriented.

FORTUNATELY, MOST MAJOR DECISIONS in our day-to-day lives don't have to be made in a split second. We normally have anywhere from minutes to months to ponder our choices. Yet, "I didn't have a choice" has become something of a catchall excuse for making bad decisions. It is, in fact, an excuse based on denial, because, as I pointed out earlier in my discussion of honesty, a person *always* has the choice of doing the right thing, even if it's a choice that is unappealing to him.

There is no worse feeling than being acutely aware that you should not be doing what you're doing, or, conversely, that you should be doing something that you aren't doing. Whenever you find yourself in this kind of situation—and all people do from time to time, even those who are generally self-disciplined—it's important to be con- scious of the fact that you have *chosen* to do the wrong thing or *chosen* not to do the right thing.

A common example of people thinking they have no choice is to be found in the previous-investment trap. Have you ever invested an inordinate amount of time, emotional energy, and/or money in a situation that didn't work out? In this respect, a bad marriage or love relationship is very much like a bad stock investment.

In either case, the attitude often is, "I've already put so much into this situation that I have no choice but to see it through." If it's the stock market, such thinking can lead to a person's losing a lot more money than he's already lost, then later wishing he had cut his losses short. If it's a marriage or love relationship, the stakes are much higher, because the cost of staying in a bad relationship can be many additional years of pain. More investment capital can always be earned; additional years, however, cannot. Time is a fixed commodity.

HIGH CLASS VERSUS LOW CLASS

Everyone wants to be considered high class, but few people take the time to think about what the term *high class* really means. For many, it translates into a big house, fancy cars, and expensive clothes. To me, however, being high class equates to having the self-discipline to consistently resist the lure of momentary pleasure in favor of actions that you believe will produce the best long-term benefits for you and your family. A low-class person, by contrast, is someone who consistently chooses instant gratification over actions geared toward reaping long-term benefits.

Thus, a high-class individual merely does, on a consistent basis, what most low-class people know is right but still choose not to do. The starting point for being high class is to *think* high class, because actions tend to follow thoughts. "Living for the moment" implies that a person has little faith in his future, while the act of foregoing comfort and pleasure today for a better life tomorrow implies a belief in one's ability to control his own destiny.

Long-term thinking is a vital key to taking rational action, because short-term pleasure can be self-destructive if not weighed against long-term consequences. If, for example, a spouse is unfaithful, it may bring him short-term pleasure, but the long-term result could be a lifetime of pain. It is self-evident that basing one's actions primarily on instant gratification is not a rational way to live one's life.

Unfortunately, as a general rule, those actions that provide the greatest amount of immediate pleasure are the very actions that are most detrimental to our long-term health, happiness, and financial success.

SEED PLANTING

Seed planting is an important high-class activity that involves the investment of time, energy, and/or money today to reap benefits tomorrow. On a daily basis, you may not notice that the seeds are slowly sprouting, but one fine day you wake up and discover that they are in full bloom. Seed planting is about laying foundations. It's about cultivating relationships. It's about planning and preparation. More than anything else, seed planting is about having the self-discipline to bypass instant gratification and take actions aimed at producing long-term success.

It's a great irony that young people, who have most of their lives in front of them, have difficulty exercising the self-discipline to plant seeds, while older folks, who are increasingly running out of time, are generally much more inclined to make good long-term choices. In fact, an excellent definition of maturity is the willingness to forego instant gratification—definitely not a teenager's strongest attribute. Why should it be when he is positively convinced of his own immortality?

Learning about computers has caused an increase in my appreciation for seed planting. I'm always surprised when I talk to someone who uses a computer yet doesn't know how to create macros or templates. These two computer functions are classic cases of the efficacy of seed planting. Anyone can learn to create macros and templates in thirty minutes or so. Once learned, a simple macro or template can be generated in a matter of seconds, a complicated one in a few minutes. The new macro or template can then be used thousands of times over a period of many years, saving untold hours of work.

Put another way, the immediate effort is measured in minutes, the long-term benefit in hours. Unfortunately, it's been my observation that most computer users don't have a clue as to how much time they could save by learning simple tasks such as creating macros and templates.

Speaking of learning, it's a seed-planting activity that pays huge dividends throughout life. I find it fascinating that the older I get, the more important learning becomes to me, yet when I was in school, learning was anathema. I wish I had studied as hard in high school and college as I do now. As a writer, I plant an enormous number of learning seeds, and much of my planting is done on something akin to blind faith; i.e., I don't know when or if I'll ever need the newly acquired knowledge, but experience has convinced me that virtually everything I learn benefits me at some future date—sometimes very far into the future.

I never cease to be amazed at how often I use information I may have acquired ten or twenty years ago. The mind is a phenomenal filing cabinet that has a way of handing you the right file when it is needed, without regard to how far in the past it may have been filed away.

LIFE MAINTENANCE

Being adept at avoiding problems is a valuable skill, because the day-to-day, unavoidable problems that we all encounter provide more of a challenge than most of us can handle. Avoiding problems is best accomplished through "life maintenance," which is really just another form of seed planting. Unlike most seed-planting activities, however, the fruits of life maintenance are to a great extent invisible. Life maintenance pays silent dividends in the form of fewer and less severe problems— what I like to refer to as the "absence-of" effect. Unfortunately, it's hard for human beings to appreciate the absence of problems, which is why all marketing experts know that prevention is a hard sell.

Following are some specific areas of life where I believe it is particularly important to practice life maintenance in an effort to avoid problems and increase one's chances of long-term success.

HEALTH
Unlike prevention, cures are easy to market. In fact, a perfect headline for an ad would be:

> I GUARANTEE I CAN CURE YOUR CANCER WITHOUT SURGERY, DRUGS, CHEMOTHERAPY, RADIATION, OR PAIN WITHIN TWO WEEKS!

Of course, the person running the ad would have to close down his boiler-room operation on short notice, convert into cash the millions of dollars in checks and credit-card payments he received, and find a way to get out of the country before being arrested. But you can be certain that thousands of people afflicted with cancer would respond to such an ad.

At the same time, we see thousands of ads, articles, and television shows every year that tell us how to *prevent* cancer—as well as heart disease, diabetes, and stroke—yet most of us choose to ignore them. That's because we don't have those diseases right now, so we aren't motivated to concern ourselves with them. It's so much easier to ignore the warnings and instead indulge ourselves with cigarettes, liquor, and unhealthy foods. After all, we can always worry about a disease when it arrives. Unfortunately, like most unpleasant events, diseases have a way of showing up when we're least prepared to cope with them.

This is why a regular medical check-up—a way of making sure that the body's machinery is all there and still working reasonably well—is an essential part of health maintenance. So, too, are proper eating and exercise, because to be of any value, they should be practiced on a regular basis, preferably daily. There is, of course, no instant gratification in any of this. Is there anything pleasurable about taking vitamins, flooding your body with juices, and eating fresh fruit for breakfast, salads for lunch, and steamed vegetables for dinner? Nevertheless, everyone is capable of taking such health-oriented actions on a regular basis. It's just a matter of self-discipline.

Of course, smoking is hands down the most destructive of all activities when it comes to body maintenance. Notwithstanding, millions of people push the health envelope by defiantly continuing to smoke. In Chapter 2, I suggested that what keeps people smoking is the dangerous self-delusion that they are immortal. While this self-delusion is on an emotional level, on an intellectual level any smoker with an IQ above thirty knows better. So what we have here is a one-two punch—a subconscious belief in immortality and a conscious lack of self-discipline. It's a one-two punch that can be quite deadly.

The fact is that people do have a choice when it comes to body-killing activities such as smoking, drug use, excessive alcohol intake, and regular consumption of foods heavily laden with saturated fat, cholesterol, salt, and sugar. We've heard many celebrities—Yul Brynner and Sammy Davis, Jr. are two well-known examples that come to mind—appeal to the public to stop smoking after they themselves were diagnosed with terminal cancer. Their appeals were noble, but it's sad that their choices to ignore body maintenance cost them their lives. When tempted to engage in a dangerous activity, I find it helpful to remember the messages of such people who have gambled on cigarettes and lost. It's comforting to realize that I have the power of choice in such matters, and that I can choose to override the temptation to engage in life-threatening activities and take actions that improve my odds of living a longer, healthier life.

CHILDREN

Right up there with health maintenance is child maintenance. Talking to children when *they* want to talk is a critical activity of parenthood. Children have a different kind of mental computer than adults. They can go long periods of time without displaying the slightest interest in talking to you, then, at the most inopportune moments, desperately feel the need to share their thoughts. It's a major mistake to fail to put aside your cooking, television program, or business papers when your child expresses a desire to have a conversation with you. If child maintenance is neglected too long, the child, to his parents' chagrin, may discover less constructive ways to satisfy the need to express himself. Always remind yourself that taking seed-planting action to talk to your child today could prevent his taking self-destructive action tomorrow that could ruin, or even end, his life.

ROUTINE

To many people, spontaneity is the ultimate symbol of freedom—do what you want, when you want, how you want. Routine—which is an integral part of life maintenance—represents a form of imprisonment to such people. Personally, I have found the opposite to be true. For me, a routine is an ongoing catharsis resulting not in imprisonment, but in freedom. When my life is in order, I have more time to work on constructive, long-term projects, not to mention more time for pleasurable activities. The more religiously one maintains a daily routine, the less his mind is clogged with petty problems, which, in turn, translates into lower stress and anxiety. In his book *Ageless Body, Timeless Mind*, Deepak Chopra lists a regular daily personal routine and regular work routine as two factors that retard the aging process.

MEDITATION/SPIRITUALITY

One of the highest priorities of a daily routine should be thinking time. By *thinking time*, I'm not talking about the kind of thinking one does at work. I'm referring to solitude, a quiet atmosphere (such as a park or a beach), and a relaxed mind. Some refer to this kind of activity as "meditation." Others call it "connecting with God." The label you assign to it is not important. Whether you're an atheist or religionist, what's important is that you have the self-discipline to fit some sort of meditation into your daily activities.

It is also important, though much more difficult, to avoid focusing too much on immediate problems during meditation sessions. Immediate problems represent the trees in your forest of possibilities, and most people are so busy pressure-cooking the problems of the moment that they simply don't have time to do creative thinking. The more you concentrate on the big picture when meditating, the better.

CONSCIOUS CHOICES

In addition to seed-planting and life-maintenance actions, there are many other areas of life where it's essential to employ self-discipline when it comes to taking action. Following are some of the areas that I have found to be of special significance in my own life, areas that require a great deal of vigilance when it comes to employing self-discipline.

THE CRUX OF THE ISSUE

By *crux of the issue*, I'm talking about the issue that is most directly related to the success or failure of a project. There are endless issues involved in every project that have little or no bearing on the final outcome.

I believe that the reason so many people are late for appointments and events is that they compulsively get sidetracked working on projects that don't have to be done right now—i.e., things that have nothing to do with the objective of getting themselves out the door and on the way to their destinations. Your bank statement is not going to decompose if you wait until you return from your appointment to reconcile it.

To ward off this problem, I've developed the habit of asking myself, "How important is the project that I'm working on?" or "How important is the project that I'm about to start working on?" Taking it to its logical extreme, an even better question is, "Does this project have to be done at all?" A task may be interesting, it may be fascinating, it may even add value to my life, but whether it warrants an investment of my time is the overriding issue.

Which points to the conclusion that the quickest way to finish a project is to simply cross it off your "to do" list. Does that sound like a vote for inaction? Not at all. On the contrary, it's a vote to *take action*—action that focuses on the highest-priority project in your life at any given time. This means refusing to allow yourself to become a slave to noncrucial matters.

All day long you make choices either to do what is most important at any given moment or to do something that is of lesser importance. If you're gainfully employed, you know all too well that there are not enough hours in a day to do everything that needs to be done in your job. That's why it's so important to spend as little time as possible on projects that have little to do with accomplishing your main objective.

People have a tendency to confuse the means with the end. You have to be vigilant about continually asking yourself why you're doing something. It's easy to get so caught up in the details of a project that you lose sight of your original objective. In Chapter 6, I discussed the problem of being enslaved by the obsession to try to make everything perfect, and pointed out that perfect is an enemy of action. It may be difficult for perfectionists to swallow, but I've learned the hard way that it's better to do a subpar job working on the right project than a great job working on the wrong project.

WHEN IT COMES TO focusing on the crux of the issue, it also helps to have the self-discipline to concentrate on doing what you do best and let others do the rest. It's easy to forget that we live in a division-of-labor society wherein it not only isn't necessary to do everything yourself, it isn't even necessary to understand how something works in order to use it. You don't need an intricate knowledge of computers to surf the Internet. You don't need to understand how television signals are transmitted to use a television set. Ditto with cars, DVD players, copying machines, and just about everything else you use in the normal course of living.

It's important to avoid working on projects that don't take advantage of your best skill set. This is where delegation comes in—delegating tasks to employees or outsourcing work that others can do much better than you. Delegation makes it easier for you to focus your actions on the crux of the issue, and at the heart of good delegation is the willingness to let go. Most people make the mistake of trying to battle their deficiencies. Instead, they should contract out their deficiencies and focusing on honing their best skills.

It usually will cost you a lot more in wasted time *not* to pay for someone else's services than it will to do something yourself that isn't your cup of tea. A perfect example of this the millions of people who have but a smattering of knowledge about computers, yet insist on trying to solve their computer problems through trial and error rather than paying a qualified technician to do the job.

Focusing on the crux of the issue is not really a complicated proposition. The more time you spend taking action on low-priority projects, the less time you have to take action on high-priority projects. A good way to look at it is that a successful person differs from an unsuccessful person by having the self-discipline to consistently do the things that *need to be done* in order to achieve his principal objective, while an unsuccessful person tends to work on lower-priority projects far too much of the time.

DISPERSED ATTENTION

Even when you become adept at focusing on your highest priority at any given time, you still have to fight the problem of dispersed attention. It's very easy to become distracted by meaningless thoughts, especially your own mind's mental chatter about petty, banal, and minor topics. How easy it is for your brain to wander toward thoughts of what else you should be doing, who slighted you last week, how you're going to clear up some bothersome financial problem, and a thousand and one other things that perpetually and randomly bombard your concentration. All these thoughts interfere with the creative process, and creativity is a crucial form of invisible action.

Anyone who has ever written a book knows that it cannot be done any other way but through controlled attention. Dispersed attention produces either a lot of unfinished books or books that *read* like the writer's attention was dispersed. I can tell you from personal experience that it would be impossible to complete a book without being vigilant when it comes to focusing. To write well, one must be intense, which can be debilitating to the brain. Writing is a lonely, ergonomically painful job, one that requires total concentration on the subject matter at hand.

In fact, the required intensity can become so great that I often find myself unconsciously searching for distractions. And guess what? I never have to look very far, because there are always more distractions than I can handle close by. There is nothing quite as stimulating as dusting your work area, sharpening pencils, or organizing your computer files.

But even if you conquer such dispersed-attention temptations, the odds are that you are often in close proximity to people who are highly skilled in the art of time wasting. I'm talking about individuals who continually inundate you with gossip, petty matters, and irrelevancies of every imaginable kind. It takes a significant amount of self-discipline not to allow such people to pull you off course.

While creative thinking is a positive form of invisible action, dispersed attention is a negative form of invisible action, and a considerable amount of self-discipline is required to nurture the former and avoid the latter.

THE OVERWHELMED SYNDROME

Priorities and dispersed attention aside, sometimes we have so many important projects to do that it's difficult to figure out, let alone focus on, the crux of the issue. As a result, we feel overwhelmed and end up doing nothing. It seems as though so much action is required that it results in our taking no action at all.

Like most people, throughout life I've wrestled hard with a sense of feeling overwhelmed by endless projects that continually demand my attention. Sometimes I feel as though I'm in a nightmare, standing in the middle of a room with no doors or windows and a hundred projects piled on tables around the perimeter, all simultaneously screaming at me, "Do me first! Do me first!" If I so much as nod in the direction of any one project, all the other projects in the room become violent and start picketing with signs that read: TORTOISE UNFAIR TO URGENT PROJECTS.

Whenever you find yourself in this situation, remember two basic realities:

First, given that time is a limited commodity, it isn't possible to get everything done. Rest assured, however, that you are not alone. To one extent or another, everyone has the same problem.

Second, ask yourself, "*Why* does everything need to be done?" It's as though we have an obsession with getting our lives perfectly organized in preparation for dying. You can spend a lifetime chasing the elusive dream of having every aspect of your life in perfect order, but to no avail. The day you die, you'll probably still have about the same number of projects left undone as you did the day you suffered your first overwhelmed attack.

With these two thoughts in mind, I've developed some simple action steps that never fail to alleviate any temporary state of paralysis I may experience as a result of feeling overwhelmed. By having the self-discipline to religiously follow these steps, I'm usually able to quickly get myself into a constructive-action mode.

Step No. 1: At the first sign of feeling overwhelmed, call time-out and mentally and physically come to a complete stop.

Step No. 2: Stand back and get a big-picture perspective of the situation. This makes it easier to objectively analyze the real—not imagined—downside consequences if you should fail to complete a project on time or fail to complete it at all. Always ask yourself, "So what?" If the downside doesn't involve death or terminal illness, it's simply not a life-or-death matter.

Step No. 3: Eliminate everything that isn't crucial to achieving your most important objectives. To accomplish this, you have to resign yourself to the reality that some people are going to be upset with you, but you can't allow yourself to be intimidated by others. It's important to be mentally prepared to make hard decisions, decisions that won't necessarily make you popular with everyone.

Step No. 4: Don't try to do everything; just do *something*. If you don't learn to take life one wave at a time, it will overwhelm you. The aphorism "the only way to eat an elephant is one bite at a time" is all too appropriate. Since it's impossible to get everything done, you should discipline yourself to prioritize. And since circumstances continually change, always consider present conditions when setting priorities, then let those priorities determine your actions.

Step No. 5: Begin. So simple, yet this is what the problem of feeling overwhelmed is all about. At some point, you have to *take action,* and the first step is almost always the hardest step—and the most crucial.

Step No. 6: Concentrate exclusively on the highest-priority project on your list, regardless of how important any other projects may be. This is where you really have to be self-disciplined. If you've already decided that something is the highest priority for you to work on right now, respect your own decision by ignoring the 7,328 other projects that you'd also like to get done. No matter how pressing the second-highest priority project is, it's not quite as urgent as the *number-one-priority* project on your list. The only way you'll ever be able to give the second-most-important project your complete attention is to first see the top-priority project all the way through to completion.

Step No. 7: Sustain your movement at a comfortable pace. I like to refer to this as the "slow, fast way." The frantic approach doesn't work. I'm often amazed at how much I manage to accomplish in an hour's time when I just calm down and work at a modest pace. The results of this philosophy show up most glaringly in a lack of mistakes, because nothing is more time consuming than having to go back and redo something. A mistake can even be fatal. Wyatt Earp apparently understood this, because his advice on gun dueling was to "take your time and aim."

Step No. 8: Don't stop until you're done. In our world of delusions, I've long been fascinated by people who have a habit of announcing that they're done with a project, yet, on closer inspection, it often turns out that they aren't even close to being done. Learn to go the last five yards—*and kick the extra point*—before telling anyone, especially yourself, that you're done.

Step No. 9: Then—and only then—move on to the next project. This is really an exclamation point on No. 8. Unless you're *completely* done—*really* done—don't start working on the next-most-important project, or, worse, on a project of even lesser importance. If you start dabbling in the next project before finishing the current one, you'll only succeed in stepping right back into the overwhelmed syndrome.

OVERCOMMITMENT

Overcommitment only exacerbates the problem of feeling overwhelmed. If you arbitrarily count life as beginning at age twenty-five (anything much before that being preparation for adulthood) and ending at age eighty, the average adult life consists of 20,075 days. However, approximately one-third of that time is spent sleeping, while another third is spent on nonproductive life essentials such as getting ready for bed, getting up in the morning, attending to health and personal hygiene, and going grocery shopping. That leaves less than 7,000 days for the average adult to do something constructive with his life.

Numbers don't lie, which is why they are a harsh reminder of just how important it is to make rational choices regarding how you spend your time. Most people go about their daily lives as though they were going to live forever, wasting time with impunity on meaningless activities. Worse, they make far too many impulsive commitments and find themselves either totally overwhelmed or unable to keep most of those commitments.

Do you clearly understand the amount of time involved in joining an organization, and will the benefits more than offset your loss of time? Do you clearly understand the amount of time involved in supporting a cause, and will the benefits more than offset your loss of time? Do you clearly understand the amount of time involved in committing to meet with someone, and will the benefits more than offset your loss of time?

Committing to meetings is an area where special vigilance is required, because today's stifling, cumbersome, CYA corporate environment has produced a generation of meeting addicts. Meetings are not a means to an end for such people; meetings are an end in themselves. To the extent you have a choice (and, unfortunately, if you're an employee, you often don't), you should opt out of as many meetings as possible.

Among other things, one of the problems with meetings is that they take time away from working on creative projects that usually represent the crux of the issue. In his classic novel *East of Eden,* John Steinbeck emphasized the connection between working alone and creativity when he explained, "Our species is the only creative species, and it has only one creative instrument, the individual mind and spirit of man. Nothing was ever created by two men. There are no good collaborations, whether in music, in art, in poetry, in mathematics, in philosophy. Once the miracle of creation has taken place, the group can build and extend it, but the group never invents anything. The preciousness lies in the lonely mind of a man."

The lonely mind of a man is precious, indeed. Surely Einstein didn't discover his theory of relativity during brainstorming sessions with fellow physicists Hubble and Humason. The equations leading to his discovery almost certainly were conceived in solitude. To be sure, there were collaborations interspersed with solitary thinking sessions, but the theory of relativity was developed by one man.

The more meetings you attend, especially meetings requested by others, the more your attention is diverted from your highest priorities. First and foremost in your mind should always be the question, "Is this meeting really necessary?" If you're serious about achieving long-term goals, you must have the self-discipline to focus on *your* priorities rather than someone else's. Nothing I have said here should be construed to mean that meetings are not important. On the contrary, meetings are a crucial form of action, so long as they are *your* meetings, i.e., meetings that have to do with furthering *your* agenda.

In this regard, never do I feel worse than when I've impulsively made a commitment, then feel obliged to follow through and make good on it even though I recognize that I shouldn't have agreed to it in the first place. The most effective way to avoid this problem is to develop the self-discipline to say *no*. Even if you think you might be interested in doing what the other person is requesting, unless you're 100 percent certain, it's a good idea to tell him that you'd like to think it over for a day or two.

That doesn't necessarily mean you're going to say no. It's just that a twenty-four- to forty-eight-hour time period can mean the difference between making an impulsive decision and making a self-disciplined decision based on a rational analysis of the facts. Again, this is not a vote for inaction; it's a vote for having the self-discipline to focus on actions that are priorities to *you.*

It has often been said that one of the most certain ways to fail is to try to please everyone, and I concur with that belief. Intimidation and guilt are major factors here, because human time thieves are adept at leaning pretty hard on their commitment targets. We've already discussed guilt, so that shouldn't be a factor in your decision-making process. Intimidation, however, can be a difficult weapon to combat. The truth of the matter is that intimidation, at its worst, borders on aggression, and you should make it a cardinal rule never to agree to anything that smacks of aggression.

Being too generous or too fast on the trigger with your *yeses* will usually result in dissipating scarce time and energy resources. The best rule to remember in this regard is: *Learn to say no politely and pleasantly, but immediately and firmly.* It's hard enough to avoid spreading yourself too thin just keeping up with the things you absolutely have to do and want to do—such as working, sleeping, exercising, reading, spending time with family, and enjoying various kinds of recreation—without committing to an excess of marginal projects in a hopeless effort to accommodate everyone.

CONVENTIONAL WISDOM

In Chapter 6, I discussed the importance of freeing yourself from peer pressure. When it comes to applying self-discipline before taking action, perhaps the most difficult test is warding off the impulse to go along with what everyone else is doing. Nowhere is this more graphically illustrated than in the stock market, especially when the crowd is headed in one direction and your intellect or common sense tells you it's the *wrong* direction.

The desire to follow the crowd is known in financial circles as the "lemming effect" (one person following another over the edge of a financial cliff), and it's a phenomenon that has fascinated students of both human nature and the stock market for centuries. As discussed in Chapter 2, the dot-com implosion that devastated millions of people was just the latest in a long line of lemming-inspired stock-market collapses. It feels good to be in the mainstream, but not when the mainstream is marching into a holocaust.

What is true for the lemming effect in the stock market is equally true for virtually all other areas of life. We are increasingly enslaved by our inherent desire to act in accordance with custom and tradition, what others think we should do, or what everyone else is doing. Our most horrific nightmare is to be caught on the outside of the House of Life and have to endure the pain of looking through the window at everyone else having fun, enjoying prosperity, and, worst of all, being accepted. Children, particularly teenagers, are obsessed with acting in ways that they believe will ensure that they will never suffer such a calamitous fate.

To take action based on what *I* believe to be right rather than on what *others* believe to be right, I find it helpful to constantly remind myself that civilization progresses as a result of the bold actions of a small minority of the earth's population. The masses don't invent light bulbs, automobiles, airplanes, or computers. They simply go along for the ride. Their god is "conventional wisdom," a mind-set rooted in their belief systems. Conventional wisdom essentially implies that because something hasn't yet been tried, it can't be done. When someone who is too naïve or ignorant to accept this doctrine takes bold action and audaciously not only tries something new, but succeeds at it, his success then becomes the foundation for a new addition to the conventional-wisdom library.

The desire to conform is nothing short of self-imposed enslavement—whether it involves fashion, investing, religion, government, or any other facet of life. It takes a tremendous amount of self-discipline not to be swayed into action by custom, tradition, or conventional wisdom. It takes even more self-discipline—and courage—to base your actions on what *you* believe to be right. If you guide your actions by the maxim "one man with courage is a majority," you're likely to be headed in the right direction most of the time.

THE ASSUMPTION TRAP

Some twenty years ago, my attorney and I had a conference call with another attorney ("Henry Dunce") representing an audio-cassette manufacturer. In the past, we had talked privately about Henry's lack of legal acumen and his penchant for irrationally defending his shoddy draftsmanship. After our conversation ended and Henry hung up, I told my attorney I needed to speak to him in private and would call him right back. He, in turn, replied, "I'm in a hurry. Why don't we just finish up our business right now. Henry's off the line."

Indeed, I had heard a click after Henry said his good-byes, and as far as I could tell there was no third-party noise on the phone, so I agreed to have our talk without first disconnecting the conference-call setup. It was reasonable to *assume* that Henry was off the line, if for no other reason than because it would have been unprofessional for him to remain on the phone without our knowledge. As my conversation with my attorney unfolded, he said, "Of course, Henry Dunce is so dense that we'll have to humor him in order to get this thing done."

Whereupon a voice—Henry's voice!—bellowed, "I am *not* dense, and I deeply resent your comment." Trust me, you don't want to hear the rest of the story. It was one of the most embarrassing moments of my life, and one that taught me a lot about carelessly making assumptions. In the ensuing twenty years, I have taken part in many conference calls where I needed to speak in private with one of the parties afterward, but, in spite of any inconvenience, I've always exercised the self-discipline to hang up and call back.

The words "I assumed" are among the most perilous in the English language, yet most people stumble through life on a road laced with land-mine assumptions, and some assumptions can be fatal. Among gun buffs, for example, when someone accidentally shoots himself, there's an old saying that he was shot by an "unloaded" gun. Of course, it's a remark that's meant to be tongue-in-cheek. No one in his right mind points a loaded gun at himself. It's almost always a case of someone *assuming* that a gun was not loaded.

The same assumption mind-set can be seen in people who cross the street with a body language that borders on arrogance. They assume that because "the pedestrian always has the right of way," cars will automatically yield to them. You've probably seen the results of such an assumption lying in the crosswalk, with a police car and ambulance close by. What an ignorant and dangerous assumption for a pedestrian to make in this day and age of epidemic drunk driving. The reason they call them *accidents* in the first place is because drivers don't always do what they're supposed to do.

Without question, my ill-fated conference call owed its bad ending to both my attorney's and my laziness. Caring is a wonderful antidote to laziness, because it's almost the antithesis of assumption. Show me someone who cares enough about what he's doing, and I'll show you someone who doesn't make many assumptions. Instead, he takes the trouble to check the facts for himself. And if it involves something of special importance, he'll step in and take matters into his own hands. A good metaphor to live by is: When the ball is on the one-yard line, never risk a fumble by handing it off to someone else; carry it over yourself.

WHO'S IN CONTROL, ANYWAY?

For reasons I don't understand, most people seem to assume that that someone, somewhere is in control of everything. This assumption is, of course, welcomed by politicians, because it's a major justification for their existence. The truth be known, however, the longer I live, the more convinced I am that *no one* is in control of *anything*. (How can anyone think otherwise when electrical grids go down for days at a time? Or terrorists are still able to carry out attacks on American soil. Or 100,000 people a year die in U.S. hospitals, not from their surgeries, but from unsanitary conditions that cause them to contract deadly bacterial infections.)

On a day-to-day level, this laziness-leading-to-assumptions syndrome continually challenges us. I've found that life becomes much easier if I override my laziness with self-discipline even when it comes to seemingly innocuous matters. A classic example of how this habit can alleviate a lot of unnecessary problems is when it comes to dealing with repairmen. How many times have you had a technician assure you that your computer not only has been repaired, but tested, only to find afterwards that it was not adequately repaired or that the repairs created a whole new set of problems?

To the considerable irritation of repairmen, I'm adamant about testing the repaired item *myself* before they leave. Invariably, the item needs more work, after which I *again* test it. This won't make you popular with technicians or service people, but it's guaranteed to lower your stress.

When you employ the self-discipline not to assume that everything you hear is true, and take action to check out the facts yourself, it's a classic example of the "slow, fast way" that I referred to earlier. Though engaging in due diligence may appear to slow you down, it actually saves you time in the long run. Nothing slows you down more than having to go back and do something over again because your original actions were based on an assumption that proved to be incorrect.

Bottom line: Assume nothing. If your mother says she loves you, check it out!

DEALING FROM STRENGTH

Always remember that it's not action we're after, but *self-disciplined* action. Undisciplined action is *disorganized* action. The last thing in the world you want to do is mistake action for direction, because if your emphasis is on action just for the sake of action, you could be moving sideways. Worse, you could be moving backwards.

It takes *intelligent* action to achieve meaningful results. Whether it's your search for truth, creating value, adhering to sound virtues, eliminating undesirable people from your life, freeing yourself from activities that imprison you, or any other noble objective, making self-disciplined choices to act in accordance with what you believe to be right is crucial to success.

In the very first sentence of Chapter 1, I said that the difference between success and failure is not nearly as great as most people might suspect. The person who succeeds and the person who fails at the same endeavor may both know how to succeed, but often there is one major difference between them: The successful person disciplines himself to rely on his intellect and do what is in his long-term best interest, while the unsuccessful person too frequently allows his emotions to prevail and gears his actions toward instant gratification.

So self-discipline is a two-step process: First, you must consistently analyze the probable, long-term consequences of your actions. Second, you must be vigilant when it comes to *acting* in accordance with what you have determined to be in your long-term best interest.

I like to refer to this as "future-oriented thinking"—the ability to connect current actions with the long-term results of those actions. It's a mistake to think of the long term as some amorphous point in the future that will never actually arrive. It will, and, worse, it has an annoying habit of arriving ahead of schedule. It's the day-in-day-out implementation of self-disciplined action that determines where you will be at the end of a week, a month, a year, and a lifetime. You can't afford to sit back and passively allow the future to creep up on you. You have to apply self-disciplined action, on a consistent basis, to be properly prepared for it.

One final word of caution: Keep in mind that if you can't muster the self-discipline to take rational action, inaction also has consequences. To the extent you are guilty of the latter, you will have no choice but to *react* to changes as they occur. But when you go on the offensive and effect beneficial changes in your life, you deal from a position of strength. There are, of course, no guarantees. Your actions could turn out to be wrong, but at least they will be your *actions* rather than your *reactions*.

CHAPTER 8

Adversity and Action

Fresh activity is the only means of overcoming adversity.

— JOHANN WOLFGANG VON GOETHE

BOB CONNELL, A HIGH school classmate of mine, was a superbly conditioned athlete who was into a healthy diet long before the general public even knew there was such a thing. He was self-confident and always appeared to be in control of his destiny. Best of all, he was a terrific guy, easygoing and friendly to everyone.

After setting swimming and track records in high school, Bob seemed headed for greatness in college. He was on the swimming team at Ohio State and doing well academically. His future looked bright. Then, one day, came the news: Trans World Airlines flight 266 had collided in midair with United Airlines flight 826 over New York City. Bodies and the wreckage of the two aircraft were strewn over a wide area of the city, with the United Airlines plane crashing into a heavily populated section of Brooklyn. It was a gruesome scene that the major networks covered in graphic detail. Shockingly, Bob Connell had been aboard the Trans World Airlines flight.

At Bob's funeral, the pastor emphasized what a full life he had lived in a relatively short period of time. He talked about the usual things that clergymen touch on when someone dies unexpectedly, and said that God had his reasons for taking such a young man so early in life. On the way out of the church, another high school classmate of mine who attended the funeral service said to me, in a bitter tone, "I don't care what the pastor says, the truth is that Bob just got screwed."

His comment has stayed with me through the years. Did Bob Connell just "get screwed," or was there a divine reason for his untimely death? In the ensuing years, I have become increasingly conscious of how so many seemingly good people become victims of harsh death or disabling injuries. Why was Ron Goldman brutally murdered when he was in the midst of doing a good deed by bringing O. J. Simpson's ex-wife, Nicole, her glasses? Why did Christopher Reeve end up a quadriplegic as a result of merely riding a horse? Each of us could make a long list of similar injustices we've observed, not only regarding people we have read and heard about, but individuals we have personally known.

The age-old question, then, is why do some people manage to miraculously escape death, while others, who seem to have everything going for them, meet with disaster early in their lives? How can a person be so unlucky as to be crushed to dust because some religious lunatics from halfway around the world decide to hijack a couple of jumbo jets and fly them into office buildings? How can life be so unjust?

Conversely, why do so many seemingly undeserving and/ or incompetent people stumble into positions of great wealth and power? Why is one man born into Great Britain's royal family while another man is born a peasant in North Korea? Though it seems grossly unjust, it is undeniable that there is an element of luck (or is it something else that we just don't understand?) when it comes to determining how people's lives turn out.

Often, timing alone seems to play a major role in determining whether a person's life ends in disaster or success. Some people become victims of grave tragedies, while others, just because they are fortunate enough to be born into a different time period, enjoy security and prosperity to an extreme. For example, professional black athletes in America today live in luxury, but their ancestors were kidnapped, sold into slavery, and spent their lives in misery.

People who were born at the wrong time in the old Soviet Union lived bleak, terror-filled lives under a brutal dictatorship, sometimes being sentenced to hard labor in the gulag, other times being put to death. Today, Russians live in a democracy (sort of), and, though the going has been shaky, individuals in that country are now reasonably free to pursue success without draconian government interference.

Jews who happened to have been living in Germany and other Nazi-occupied European countries during Hitler's reign of terror experienced an even worse fate. But today, Jews are free and, on average, are perhaps the most prosperous ethnic group in the world. Likewise, people living in Hiroshima or Nagasaki in 1945 became victims of the first atomic bombs dropped on civilian populations, but today Japan is a free and affluent society.

GOD AND EVIL

When we witness or read about gross injustice, it raises the age-old spiritual and philosophical question: Why does God allow "evil" and/ or injustice to exist?

A fatalist, be he an atheist or religionist, would tend to believe that injustice is predetermined. In the case of the atheist, however, an injustice really represents a random event; i.e., the fact that it was predetermined by the so-called Big Bang is pretty much irrelevant, because he still had no knowledge that it was going to occur. A religionist, however, might tend to believe that an injustice is the work of God, possibly as a punishment for some wrongdoing. The reason for the injustice is not always clear to him, though it's possible that it may become clear at some future date. If not, the religionist can also choose to believe that the reason for the injustice will become clear in the afterlife.

A *Time* magazine article some years ago reflected on the *Why?* question. If God exists, the author rhetorically asked, why does he permit evil in the world? The article alluded to such perceived evils as Hitler's attempted extermination of the Jews, the then-recent cyclone in Bangladesh, and Pol Pot's use of the Khmer Rouge to kill some 2 million Cambodians. More current examples would include the genocide perpetrated against Croatian citizens by former Yugoslavian president Slobodan Milošević, suicide bombings bombings and aimed at Israeli civilians by terrorist organizations such as Hamas and Hezbollah, and the dozens of people injured or killed in the Boston Marathon bombings.

The article thrashed over much of the same ground covered in Harold Kushner's landmark book *When Bad Things Happen to Good People*. Forced to reconcile his belief in God with his son's tragic death from the incurable, rapid-aging disease progeria, Rabbi Kushner arrived at the interesting conclusion that God is all-loving but not omnipotent. Though it would be impossible for most of us to view this topic from Rabbi Kushner's perspective, I am compelled to say that, for me, it is spiritual fudging to take the position that God is a good guy, but impotent. Either God is all-knowing and all-powerful, or He is not God.

The *Time* article paraphrased theologian Frederick Buechner in pointing out the dilemma that you can match any two of the following propositions, but never all three: (1) God is all powerful. (2) God is all good. (3) Terrible things happen.

In George Smith's book *Atheism: The Case Against God*, he states the dilemma in more detail by writing, "Briefly, the problem of evil is this: If God does not know there is evil, he is not omniscient. If God knows there is evil but cannot prevent it, he is not omnipotent. If God knows there is evil and can prevent it but desires not to, he is not omnibenevolent. If . . . God is all-knowing and all-powerful, we must conclude that God is not all-good. The existence of evil in the universe excludes this possibility."

To Smith's persuasive list, however, I would add one other possibility: Perhaps God knows there is evil in the world, but does not choose to stop it for reasons that are beyond our understanding. In other words, God alone knows why He does what He does. If God exists, He is unknowable and undefinable by human standards. *That,* after all, is what makes him God.

The *Time* article goes on to say that, "Perhaps man is to God as the animals of the earth are to man. . . . Can it be that God visits evils upon the world not out of perversity or a desire to harm, but because our suffering is a by-product of his needs?" Well put. However, to extend this analogy and look at it in a slightly different light, consider the possibility that man is to God as a dog is to man, and a dog is to man as a flea is to a dog; i.e., the man, the dog, and the flea, who are merely tagging along for the ride, have neither the faintest idea as to why their masters do what they do nor the means to ever understand why.

The question then becomes: Is God indifferent to us, as the dog is to the flea, or does He allow us to suffer for reasons we do not understand? When someone takes his dog to the veterinarian, the dog has no idea why his master allows pain to be inflicted on him. In the same way, perhaps God doesn't always give us what we want, but what He knows we need.

One could even take the position that it's the height of arrogance to suggest that we should be able to understand evil and suffering, let alone make judgments about the actions of a Supreme Power. If there is a God, surely He operates in a completely different dimension than we do, thus He alone knows His purpose. So, even though *Atheism: The Case Against God* is an undeniably brilliant book, its impeccable logic is rendered irrelevant if God does, in fact, exist; i.e., Smith's logic is valid only in a *secular* dimension. A Supreme Power would transcend secular knowledge, just as man transcends a dog's capacity to understand human reasoning.

In any event, it would be inconsistent to believe in God, yet question perceived evil and injustice. Only God can know the reasons for the existence of evil and injustice. Of course, if one is an atheist, he has no choice but to accept random evil and injustice as natural aspects of life. Either way, the most profound search for truth will never yield a conclusive answer to the question of why evil and injustice exist. It makes sense, then, to accept evil and injustice as normal components of life and do the best you can to stack the odds in your favor by focusing your efforts on those areas over which you have control.

Clearly, one of the toughest things about life is that nothing is certain. You can do everything right—lead an action-filled, self-disciplined life based on truth and sound virtues—yet have all your efforts offset by one bad break. The truth of the matter is that life can, indeed, be unjust. Does that mean we should just give up and accept predestination as all-controlling? I think not. As discussed earlier, the evidence seems clear that even though we may not be able to change those things that are inevitable, human history appears to make it self-evident that we have the capacity to shape a great deal of our destiny. This capacity, I believe, stems from our ability to take action, which, along with the help of the Cosmic Catalyst, produces the genius, magic, and power necessary to convert our dreams into physical realities.

As Benjamin Disraeli put it, "Man is not the creature of circumstances, circumstances are the creature of man. We are free agents, and man is more powerful than matter."

THE BLAME GAME

Injustice aside, it is not uncommon for an individual to fail to recognize that what he perceives as a bad break is really nothing more than the natural consequences of his own actions. When this occurs, the individual is a victim not of injustice, but an illusion. In medical terminology, such an illusion is known as *transference*, the act of looking to others, or to circumstances perceived to be beyond one's control, for the source of one's problems.

In real terms, it means that the individual has conceded defeat, because he cannot solve problems over which he has no control. It's somewhat analogous to brainwashing, though in the case of transference a person actually brainwashes himself in an effort to avoid accountability. In most cases, it is not injustice that's the culprit; it is one's own bad choices.

It would be appropriate to refer to this as the Blame Game, a game in which individuals blame circumstances, conditions, or other people for their behavior and/or results. The Blame Game is at the wrong end of the action spectrum. It destroys self-confidence and strips the afflicted individual of his motivation to take action to solve his problems.

Even when someone does something dishonest that causes you harm, you do yourself no favor by blaming your troubles on him. Blaming the other person is a bad habit that can spread like a cancer to all areas of your life and become an excuse for failure, while an inward-looking approach to analyzing an unpleasant event in your life can pave the way for future success.

There's a difference between engaging in transference and making an honest attempt to analyze the cause of a problem. There is always a *reason* for a bad consequence, but a reason is different from an *excuse*. An excuse implies an attempt to escape accountability. The fact that someone may have been dishonest with you might be a legitimate *reason* why you were harmed, but if you use the other person's dishonesty as an *excuse* for what happened to you, you are letting yourself off the hook and thereby escaping personal responsibility.

In the above case, the best long-term solution would be to learn from the bad experience and work at becoming more adept at "reading" people. No matter what someone else did to you, it's in your best interest to ask yourself what *you* can do to avoid dealing with such an individual in the future, which is something that is, to a great extent, within your control. The best thing about the latter approach is that it isn't dependent upon your ability to get someone to admit that he's wrong or to make reparations to you—which is good, because history teaches us that the possibility of either of these things occurring is extremely remote.

You should therefore never release yourself from accountability, regardless of the circumstances in any given situation. It's *always* in your best interest to look in the mirror for the cause of your problems, because the guy looking back at you is the only person over whom you will ever have total control. By analyzing a problem from the standpoint of what *you* could have done to avoid it in the first place, you are in a position to take action to avoid its recurrence. This requires intellectual honesty and a willingness to subordinate your delicate ego to the pursuit of long-term success.

THE ILLUSION OF ADVERSITY

Even if one's perception of the facts is accurate, it is still possible to misread an event or circumstance as an adversity or setback. The problem is that we tend to judge events on the basis of their immediate impact, but, as life repeatedly teaches us, the long-term consequences of an action can be quite different from what we initially observe. The bad is superficial and obvious; the good often takes investigation and long-term observation. It's important to recognize that the true result of an event may take a long period of time to come to fruition.

Thus, misfortune and setbacks are frequently nothing more than illusions, which is why we so often fail to connect the long-term benefits to the seemingly negative situation that confronts us. The truth is that adversity can serve as both a learning experience and a masked opportunity. In fact, I would take it one step further and say that there is an offsetting opportunity in every adversity, every obstacle, and every injustice.

The trick is to develop the habit of automatically looking for the positive in every negative situation. It took me years to develop this habit, but now, even when something seemingly terrible occurs, I immediately take a deep mental breath and start thinking about where the Cosmic Catalyst is trying to lead me. Some of the unexpected roads this practice takes me down are nothing less than miraculous.

A classic example of this phenomenon that is especially dear to my heart is the story of how my first book was rejected by twenty-three publishers. It was obvious that some of the publishers didn't even take the trouble to look at my manuscript, and simply returned it with form letters of rejection. Others sent customized letters, many of which were brutally candid in telling me why my book was unsaleable.

While I won't deny that some of the stinging comments put a dent in my self-confidence, I was passionate about what I had written, and I had a burning desire to get the book into the hands of the public. So, in desperation, I decided to publish it myself, even though I had zero knowledge of the book-publishing business. In fact, it would have been impossible to have been less prepared than I was to publish a book. I certainly was not about to spend a couple of years learning the intricacies of the book-publishing business, which, as it turned out, can only be learned through experience, anyway.

So, ignorance aside, something compelled me to take action. After I had 5,000 copies of my book printed up, a remarkable thing happened: My bold (some referred to it as audacious) action resulted in an explosive expansion of my mental paradigm, though at the time I didn't even know what a paradigm was. I became resourceful beyond anything I previously would have thought possible and went *way* beyond the boundaries of so-called conventional wisdom.

Though I had no advertising experience, I decided to run ads in local newspapers and the *Wall Street Journal*. The first ad I ran, in the *San Antonio Express-News*, produced such poor results that I lost 90 percent of my advertising investment. I was shaken, but not deterred. I sprang back into action and worked hard at analyzing what was wrong with my first ad. Then, based on my analysis, I rewrote the ad and ran it in the *Wall Street Journal*. The result was an early lesson in the importance of both choosing the right medium and coming up with the right ad copy, because my second attempt resulted in a huge success with sales nearly double the cost of the ad.

I soon worked my way up to full-page ads, and continued to run those ads in the *Wall Street Journal* for about nine months. This resulted in sales of about 60,000 books and, more important, brought me a lot of attention. The attention brought calls from Brentano's (the most prestigious bookstore in New York City at the time), which offered to buy large quantities of my book if I would agree to put its name at the bottom of one of my ads; from Thomas Y. Crowell (later acquired by Harper & Row), which made a proposal to distribute my book to bookstores nationwide; and from Fawcett Publications (later acquired by Ballantine Books), which offered me what, at the time, seemed like an obscene sum of money to publish the book in paperback.

The book, *Winning through Intimidation*, ultimately climbed to #1 on the *New York Times* Best-Seller List, which turned out to be the first of a string of bestsellers for me. There is absolutely no doubt in my mind that none of this would have happened had my book *not* been rejected by every publisher I submitted it to, because, as I subsequently learned through experience, 99 percent of books published by mainstream publishers—particularly major publishers—get zero advertising and little, if any, publicity.

So, what initially appeared to be an enormous adversity was, in fact, a great opportunity. All that was required of me was to apply action and resourcefulness to an apparent obstacle, and the long-term result shocked the publishing industry.

I've repeated this same lemons-to-lemonade trick so often over the years that I've lost count of the number of times that seemingly major obstacles have turned out to be great opportunities in disguise, just waiting to be exploited. And the more I've done it, the more I've learned. Best of all, each new learning experience makes it that much easier the next time around.

INTERESTINGLY, THE PHENOMENON OF short-term illusions is as true for good breaks as it is for bad ones. As a person makes his way through life's peaks and valleys, he often finds that getting the sweetheart, job, or opportunity he believed he always wanted can turn out to be the worst thing that could have happened to him. So, just as there are always offsetting positives in every negative situation, there also are offsetting negatives in every positive situation. In truth, virtually every experience we have is both good and bad, so the secret is to develop the habit of focusing on the positive aspects of every situation.

In truth, for every positive, there's an offsetting negative, and for every negative, there's an offsetting positive.

PERSPECTIVE

In 1987, while on a seminar tour, I happened to be staying overnight in Houston. After a particularly tiring, stressful day, I made an appointment for a massage at the health spa in the hotel where I was staying. By the time my appointment rolled around, I was in a pretty gruff mood and looking forward to having someone work on my tired body.

As I finished putting my clothes in a locker and wrapping a towel around my waist, a spa worker greeted me and asked that I follow him to my assigned massage room. It crossed my mind as a bit unusual that the masseur himself did not come out to greet me, but, being exhausted and stressed, I didn't give it too much thought.

After entering the massage room, the masseur introduced himself, shook my hand, and asked me to lie face down on the table. As I began to get onto the massage table, I happened to notice that the masseur was staring straight ahead. I immediately did a mental double take and was instantly jolted out of my own little myopic world. It was evident that the masseur ("Paul") was blind.

I soon felt comfortable enough to ask him if he had been blind all his life. "No," Paul responded, "it happened about thirty years ago, when I was nineteen years old." He went on to explain that he was planning to become a doctor, and was attending a summer orientation session at a special training school in Oklahoma for a few weeks. He became friendly with another young man ("Charles"), who took him into his confidence and told him about a lucrative scam he was operating. Charles explained that he had a ring of college students cashing counterfeit bank checks he printed up and was giving them a percentage of the take.

After a time, Charles asked Paul if he would like to get in on the deal. Paul immediately told him that he wasn't interested, and thought that would be the end of the matter. But later that night, Charles came to Paul's motel room and pulled a gun on him. He told Paul that he had no choice but to kill him, because he knew too much about his illegal activities. Without even giving him an opportunity to promise that he would never mention it to anyone, the man shot Paul in the head. He assumed he was dead, and left him lying on the floor in a pool of blood.

The bullet had severed Paul's right optic nerve, and he was later told that his left eye could have been saved had he been taken to a hospital right away. Instead, he lay on the floor for eighteen hours before he was found, and blood clotting and other complications caused him to lose the sight in his left eye as well. In a voice of resignation that I will never forget, Paul concluded his tragic story by saying, "And I've been blind ever since."

I suddenly found myself thinking of all the things I take for granted that Paul had never experienced. In his entire adult life, he hasn't seen a beautiful tree, a spectacular sunset, or a magnificent painting. Lying on the massage table, my fatigue and stress seemed to fade away as these sobering thoughts pervaded my mind. How right Socrates was when he said, "If all our misfortunes were laid in one common heap whence everyone must take an equal portion, most people would be contented to take their own."

My experience with the blind masseur in Houston had a major effect on my life by helping me to keep perceived problems, injustices, and adversities in proper perspective. By *perspective*, I'm talking about the capacity to view things on their relative level of importance. When someone loses his job, he may feel as though the world were coming to an end. But if he loses his health, his perspective changes and he just wishes his only problem was not having a job.

One of the main reasons human beings have such a difficult time keeping perceived problems in perspective is because they tend to take themselves too seriously. But it's possible to rise above this tendency, because, unlike animals, a human being possesses the capacity to transcend himself, i.e., the ability to detach himself both from situations and from his own self. He can choose not to see every problem, every injustice, and every adversity as a life-or-death matter.

In other words, we have been given the ability to view our problems in a relative light. Not every bad break turns out to be bad in the long run; not every problem is a bona fide injustice; and not every injustice is major when juxtaposed against the millions of injustices that occur daily throughout the world. To paraphrase Charles Dickens's first paragraph in *A Tale of Two Cities*: It was the best of times; it was the worst of times; it was, in fact, pretty much like any other time.

Which is to say that crises come and go, but only one time in history is the world going to come to an end—and one thing about which you can be certain is that you won't be around to remember it happening anyway.

HANDICAPS

A healthy perspective has allowed me to view so-called physical handicaps in a different light since my daughter was diagnosed with multiple sclerosis at a relatively young age. Like most parents confronted with the illness of a child, I went through the usual stages of denial, anger, and despair. However, as the years passed, I increasingly focused on how lucky my daughter was that she did not have chronic-progressive multiple sclerosis. People with the latter form of multiple sclerosis deteriorate rather quickly, and usually become confined to a wheelchair early on. My daughter, who is attractive, intelligent, and personable, has been able to lead a relatively normal life, raise two children, and continue on a successful career path.

Knowing that there are millions of people much worse off than my daughter has had a positive effect on both of us. Even more positive are the endless stories of severely disabled people who have enjoyed great success and managed to live meaningful, vital lives by taking action to overcome their handicaps. Following are four of my favorite examples:

Tom Dempsey, born without a right hand and with half of his right foot missing, played eleven seasons in the National Football League as a place kicker, making 159 of 258 field goal attempts. All this would have been amazing enough in itself, but the most remarkable part of his story is not only that he did his kicking with his deformed right foot, but he also kicked the longest field goal in NFL history—63 yards (later tied, in 1998, by Jason Elam of the Denver Broncos)—to beat the Detroit Lions in a game in 1970 with no time left on the clock. Dempsey remembers how his father used to tell him, "You can do anything you want to do. You may have to do it differently, but you can do it." Translation: If you expand your mental paradigm and become resourceful enough, anything is possible.

In 1983, Art Berg, an athletic young entrepreneur with his whole life in front of him, was involved in a tragic automobile accident that left him a quadriplegic. After his accident, one doctor told him that it was important for him to come to grips with the reality that he would never get married, have children, or be employable.

The doctor was wrong. Instead, Berg turned his unthinkable tragedy into an opportunity. He married his high school sweetheart, had two children, and became an award-winning salesman for a national firm. He later went into the bookstore business, and was recognized by the Small Business Administration as "Young Entrepreneur of the Year."

Finally, in 1991, he decided to become a motivational speaker, and spoke for free hundreds of times just to get started. That led to his becoming a $2 million-a-year motivational speaker, and he ultimately was inducted into the Motivational Speakers Hall of Fame.

Along the way, Berg also managed to find the time and determination to become an outstanding wheelchair athlete, and participated in tennis, swimming, and wheelchair rugby, to name but a few of his athletic endeavors.

Sadly, Art passed away in 2002. Perhaps his legacy is best summed up in his words, "I thank God that life is hard, because in the pain, the struggle, the loneliness, and the rejection, we begin to learn. And when we learn, we grow, and when we grow, a miracle happens. We begin to change. . . . While the difficult takes time, the impossible just takes a little longer."

Irishman Ronan Tynan was born with deformed legs, which caused him to suffer from severe scoliosis. It got so bad that at age twenty he made the breathtaking decision to have both of his legs amputated below the knees and wear prosthetic lower limbs. That could have been the end of his dreams, but, instead, it was the beginning of one of the most action-oriented lives imaginable.

Tynan set his sights on athletics, and went into serious training. From 1981 to 1984, he won eighteen gold medals and set fourteen world records competing in events for the disabled. These feats alone would have made for an incredible inspiration story, but he was just getting started.

He next made the decision to become a medical doctor, and enrolled at Trinity University in Dublin, Ireland. At thirty-two, Tynan began practicing medicine, which one would have thought would have put an exclamation point on his huge capacity to overcome adversity. Not even close.

Having discovered that he had a gifted tenor voice, in his spare time he took up singing in pubs. In 1994, he entered a television talent show in Ireland—and won! He soon gave up the practice of medicine and became a world-famous stage performer. Still, Tynan's trials and triumphs had not all been written.

As a result of a sinus-drainage problem caused by the return of a childhood injury he had suffered, he suddenly lost his voice and, reluctantly, returned to the practice of medicine. But after a long period of recuperation following surgery to correct the problem, he slowly regained his magnificent voice.

Today, he thrills audiences throughout the world with his stirring performances, and, still in his early fifties, is a relatively young man. Where he goes from here is anybody's guess, but he already has had a major impact on millions of lives, and mere mortals like myself are deeply grateful to him for the inspiration he has provided through his astonishing successes.

Most of us have had a personal relationship with at least one handicapped individual whose success has been a great inspiration to us. My favorite story in this regard is about my longtime friend Jim Blanchard. Whenever I suspect that I might unconsciously be feeling a bit sorry for myself, I think about Jim to get myself back on track.

As a teenager, Jim was tall and handsome, and he believed in individualism at an age when most kids don't even know what the word means. One evening during his senior year in high school in New Orleans, Jim and two of his buddies were drinking heavily at a dance, then made the mistake of driving when they left. It was raining heavily, and there were no seat belts to speak of in those days.

One of Jim's friends was behind the wheel, doing what teenagers usually do when they're drunk: speeding. Flying down St. Charles Avenue at seventy miles an hour, the car failed to negotiate a curve in the road, flew up in the air, and slammed into an oak tree. Jim, who had been in the backseat of the car, was catapulted through the air like a human cannonball. His flight came to an abrupt halt when his body hit a light pole at full speed. In that instant, at the tender age of seventeen, Jim's life was forever changed.

He vividly recalled a priest giving him his last rites at the scene of the accident, but that proved to be premature. Jim woke up in the hospital, and immediately knew something was very wrong. He had no feeling in either of his legs. An intern broke the news to him that his spinal cord had been severed in three places and that he would never walk again.

When Jim finally came home, he found two understandably doting parents who wanted to do everything possible to make him comfortable. Though he loved his parents dearly, their overprotectiveness bothered him a great deal, so much so that he decided he had to prove to himself that he could become independent.

He had heard about a special program in Mexico where paraplegics and quadriplegics could share houses together and learn to become self-sufficient. After some investigation, he made the decision to go to Mexico and begin the long process of turning his life around.

In Mexico, living with four other men who also were in wheelchairs, he learned to take care of his personal needs. When he returned to New Orleans after five months, having proven that he could be self-sufficient, he was anxious to get on with his life. He finished his senior year of high school, then earned a college degree.

The rest of Jim's story could fill a book, because he lived an action-packed life that would be difficult for most people to imagine. In 1971, he invested fifty dollars in a coin business, which he ultimately sold for enough millions to make him independently wealthy for life.

Jim traveled more than anyone I've ever known, and did just about anything and everything one could imagine. When a mutual friend told me that he and Jim had gone mountain climbing, I asked him how that was possible. He responded, "Because Jim doesn't understand that he's crippled." No sentence could have described the essence of Jim Blanchard any better. His being a paraplegic was just a fact to him, not a liability. Mountain climbing, like so many of the things he did, was difficult, but *not* impossible.

When an indescribably painful event intervenes in a person's life, as it did in Jim Blanchard's, he has two choices: He can feel sorry for himself and give up or he can get mad and move forward with increased determination. Jim recognized that it's your mind, not your body, that makes the decision to pick yourself up, brush yourself off, and continue to take action in the face of overwhelming odds. He may not have been able to pick himself up physically, but he instinctively knew that nothing could stop him from picking himself up mentally.

I'm sure that if Jim could have had the power to undo the terrible accident that forever changed his life, he would have done so, but he knew that wasn't an option. So, rather than fighting reality, he accepted the hand he was dealt and, in fact, told me that he often wondered whether he would have been as successful had he never been in that fateful accident many years earlier.

On March 20, 1999, after a vital, happy, prosperous life, Jim Blanchard—the personification of action—died unexpectedly in his sleep at age fifty-five. I will always miss him.

Inspirational stories like those I have just described abound by the thousands. From Helen Keller and Franklin D. Roosevelt to Stevie Wonder and Stephen Hawking, the evidence is clear that physical handicaps—the epitome of injustice—can be overcome. Always keep in mind that a handicap is just a disadvantage that makes success more difficult, but there is a clear difference between *difficult* and *impossible*.

I hasten to add that a seriously disabled person would be justified if he felt that because I myself do not have a major physical disability, I shouldn't be pontificating on the subject and giving motivational speeches about how to overcome such adversities. And perhaps he would be right. In all honesty, I cannot say for certain how I would react to losing my eyesight, becoming a quadriplegic, or having a limb removed, so I would not want my comments to come across as cavalier motivational hype.

On the contrary, I am in awe of those who have accomplished great things by overcoming major physical disabilities. It is *their* success, *their* stories, and *their* words that have inspired me to say what I have said here. They not only help me keep my own perceived problems in perspective, they reinforce my belief in the power of the partnership between action and the Cosmic Catalyst. They reaffirm my belief in the phenomenal genius, magic, and power that bold action is capable of producing.

Technically speaking, a handicap is not just a physical disability, but any kind of disadvantage that makes life more difficult. Indeed, over time I have come to realize that every person in the world has at least one bona fide handicap. An obese person has a handicap; a person with attention deficit disorder has a handicap; a person with a low IQ has a handicap; a person with big ears has a handicap; a person who comes from a poverty-stricken background has a handicap.

Handicaps can be developed after birth or can enter one's life in the form of an inherited environment. A dislikable personality is a developed handicap; an abusive parent is an inherited-environment handicap.

You, too, have a handicap; in fact, you probably have many handicaps. I don't know what they are, but I know you have them. Everyone you meet, in spite of how successful or happy he may appear to be, has a cross to bear. No one makes it through life without experiencing the hardship caused by a handicap, and each of us is faced with choosing between three alternatives when it comes to dealing with our handicaps:

1. We can roll over and die, figuratively or literally.
2. We can go through life in a perpetual state of anger, turning people off and virtually ensuring a life of misery and failure.
3. We can make a conscious decision to expand the boundaries of our mental paradigms, take inventory of the assets we have, then move forward with bold action to exploit those assets to our advantage.

As thousands of inspirational stories about overcoming adversity have demonstrated, the third alternative makes the most sense to a rational individual. One thing we know for certain is that we can't go back to the Cosmic Catalyst and ask that the cards be reshuffled. We can, however, make a conscious decision to play the cards we've been dealt to the best of our abilities. In the final analysis, it always comes down to what you *do* with what you *have*.

THE DAILY CARES OF LIFE

Other than terminal illness, accidental death, or a dire situation such as being in a concentration camp, there are few obstacles in life that can prevent you from transforming your dreams into reality through the genius, magic, and power of action. Whether or not you take action in the face of adversity is determined by your thought processes. You don't succeed by focusing on your handicaps; you succeed by focusing on your strengths. Concentrate on the abundance in your life rather than the problems, and take action to exploit that abundance. Discover your best assets, nurture them, and use them as they were meant to be used.

In reality, injustices, adversities, problems, misfortunes, and obstacles are nothing more than words we use to negatively describe our perception of a fact or set of facts. When you think about it, it doesn't even make sense to give negative labels to any set of circumstances. I prefer to think of most so-called problems as "the daily cares of life," because life is an endless stream of stumbles, inconveniences, and aggravating people who cross your path and slow you down. But since these things are rarely life-threatening, it's healthy to view them as nothing more than rites of passage.

The reality is that day-to-day "problems" are a natural, integral part of the living experience. Fortunately, most problems are not of major importance, let alone terminal in nature. So, the first step toward overcoming obstacles is to stop seeing them as "injustices," "adversities," and "problems." It's not just a matter of language. More important is that you not even think of an occurrence or situation as a problem, but, rather, as just one of those daily cares of life that requires your attention. Taking quick, efficient action to handle the daily cares of life is second in importance only to your ability to take swift, continuous action toward achieving your primary goals.

Just as it is essential to recognize that there is no such thing as success without adversity, it's important to understand that there is no such condition as defeat that can thrust itself upon you without your consent. We merely use the label *defeat* to describe the fact that we have made the decision to stop trying.

The nice thing about it is that there are no laws to limit the number of times you can try, and no special education, license, or skill required to employ perseverance. Perseverance is the ultimate action tool, a tool so powerful that it can overcome almost any kind of adversity. Perseverance is nothing more than persistent action—continuing to take action in the face of massive rejection, massive disappointment, and massive frustration.

In particular, the capacity to deflect rejection and forge ahead as though it were nothing but a minor irritant is the key to ensuring that the Law of Averages will deliver positive results. In theory, giving up is never rational, because the Law of Averages makes ultimate success a certainty. On top of that, with the help of the Cosmic Catalyst, we have the power to intervene in the Law of Averages and thereby increase our chances of success.

I suppose there could be circumstances that would cause a rational person to conclude that the odds are so long and the struggle ahead so difficult that he is no longer willing to continue on. This often happens with terminally ill people, and those of us who are more fortunate are in no position to question such decisions. I would only say that even in cases of terminal illness, many of us have known someone who miraculously managed to escape death for a long period of time by not giving up.

This subject is above mortal man's level of understanding, because it gets into that gray area of which things are predestined and which things can be altered through action and the aid of the Cosmic Catalyst. Again, however, most of the adversities we face are not life-or-death matters, and, with few exceptions, bold action can overcome everyday adversities. If you truly understand and believe there is balance in the universe, it should motivate you to quickly and automatically look for the offsetting positive in every negative situation. One way of looking at it is that every perceived problem is nothing more than an illusion hiding something of value to you.

SOMEWHAT IRONICALLY, BUT SADLY, my classmate who said that our mutual friend Bob Connell "just got screwed" by being on the wrong airplane at the wrong time ended up taking his own life some years later. While it would be a leap to suggest that an obsession with injustice was the motivating factor in his suicide, I have often wondered if his anger over Bob's unjust fate wasn't indicative of a mind too focused on the negative side of life. It makes no sense to concentrate on things that are beyond one's control, given that those things that *are* within one's control are more than a full-time job.

I recognize that some people have reputations for leading charmed lives, and that everything always seems to fall into place for them. However, my experience over the decades has convinced me that even though some individuals are dealt unusually good hands, no one makes it through life without experiencing his share of adversity. (Could there be a better example of this than the tragedy-saturated lives of the Kennedy clan?)

More often than not, having the persistence to take positive action in the face of massive injustice and adversity is the major determinant in how one's life plays out. In the words of Voltaire, "Life is thickly sown with thorns, and I know no other remedy than to pass quickly through them. The longer we dwell on our misfortunes, the greater is their power to harm us."

Thanks to inspirational people like my friend Jim Blanchard, the way I view injustice has dramatically changed over time. I have proven to my satisfaction that action is by far the best antidote to adversity. I know that fate sits on the other side of the table of life plotting future injustices, and I now recognize that it's not a question of whether I will experience adversity, but how I handle it when it makes its appearance—and what I learn from it to apply to other situations—that will decide the course of my life.

Above all, I have learned that adversity is the one factor that should *never* be used as an excuse for *not* taking action. On the contrary, it is the single most important reason for *taking* action—purposeful, con-sistent, bold action. Ironically, then, adversity is life-giving because it's a call to action—and action *is* life.

CHAPTER 9

The Endgame of Action: Happiness

Action may not always bring happiness, but there is no happiness without action.

— BENJAMIN DISRAELI

MAN HAS PROBABLY DISCUSSED happiness more than any other subject, more even than love. Both subjects are difficult to define, but there is one major difference between the two. Love is an emotion; happiness is a state of mind. Love, we are safe to assume, always produces happiness, but happiness can result from many things other than love.

If we are to make inroads into achieving happiness, we first have to understand what it is. And to do that, we need a starting point. Anyone can choose to define happiness to suit himself, but the dictionary words that are most meaningful to me are "characterized by pleasure," with pleasure, in turn, being defined as "a feeling of being pleased." (I would also point out that, just as heat, scientifically speaking, is the absence of cold, pleasure could arguably be defined as the absence of pain.) For the purposes of this book, I have used as the definition of happiness, "a state of mind characterized by a feeling of pleasure."

What, other than love, can lead to happiness? Just about anything. Caring for the poor and sick made Mother Teresa happy; i.e., it gave her pleasure to ease the pain of others. Henry Ford, on the other hand, derived pleasure from mass-producing automobiles. Which of these two did more to make *others* happy is a subject open to debate, but it has nothing to do with the fact that both of them took action that they believed would result in their experiencing the greatest amount of pleasure and least amount of pain. What they had in common was that they were human, and human beings are genetically programmed to gravitate toward pleasure and avoid pain. What they did not have in common was a singular method for achieving happiness.

Regardless of how strange or offensive we may find the actions of other people to be, *their* happiness is not about our feelings. It's about *their* feelings. It's about what gives *them* pleasure. Who am I to tell you what makes you happy? Who are you to tell me what makes me happy? Clearly, each of us seeks happiness in our own way.

It is the height of arrogance to try to tell others what should make them happy, yet politicians and self-styled moralists are obsessed with doing just that. Worse, political-action groups take it one step further, trying to achieve their happiness by appealing to the government to use force against those who don't agree with their positions.

If no one else can tell you what makes you happy, then neither can anyone tell you whether or not you *are* happy. Only you know how much pleasure and pain you feel inside. One good way to measure your feelings of pleasure and pain is to take note of how often you find yourself choosing among good alternatives and how often you find yourself choosing among the lesser of two (or more) bad alternatives. When you choose between bad alternatives, you are not choosing to eliminate pain, but only to ease as much pain as possible. If you find yourself choosing among painful alternatives too often, you're probably not doing a very good job of searching for truth.

If achieving happiness is the endgame of action, then rational actions are those that have the best chance of producing *the greatest amount of happiness over the long term*. Marilyn Monroe was probably happy for a while; Janis Joplin was probably happy for a while;

John Belushi was probably happy for a while. Happiness was not the problem for any of these celebrities or millions of other people who have come to an early dead end in life. It's *long-term* happiness that was the problem for them. High-class people make decisions geared to future happiness; low-class people make decisions geared to instant, usually short-lived happiness.

I suppose even a serial killer could experience momentary happiness, but his actions almost certainly would result in long-term *un*happiness. In fact, he probably would experience an enormous amount of mental pain between murders, in which case his happiness would be very short lived. In any event, a serial killer would be way out of line morally, because he would be achieving his happiness through an extreme form of aggression against others.

The good news is that making decisions geared toward long-term happiness does not preclude one from being happy in the short term as well. What it does mean is that a person should not consistently opt for instant gratification without regard to the long-term consequences of his actions. It's unwise to compartmentalize one's life into the present and future; rather, the two components should be viewed as inextricably entwined. To the extent that one makes instant-gratification decisions that are in conflict with his long-term happiness, such decisions will usually prove to be self-destructive.

CHASING HAPPINESS

I've always felt that the dumbest question anyone can ask another person is, "Are you happy?" Yet, it's an old favorite of media people when interviewing celebrities. What makes the question so eminently stupid is the fact that even if there were such thing as absolute happiness, there would be no accurate way of quantifying it. Theoretically, you can be happier every day of your life than you were the day before. The gradations are infinite. You can accidentally shoot yourself in the foot, lose your little toe, and be happy that you didn't lose your big toe. Losing your little toe is a painful thing to think about, while not losing your big toe is a pleasant thing to think about.

Our modern-day obsession with happiness has millions of people all over the world chasing their happiness tails. In truth, however, it's a mistake to dwell on happiness. In fact, there are few things that can be a greater obstacle to happiness than focusing on happiness to an excess. As explained earlier, paradoxical intention is a phenomenon whereby we decrease our chances of achieving something if we dwell on it too much. As Viktor Frankl explained, "Happiness . . . cannot be pursued . . . [T]he more we aim at it, the more we miss our aim." If there is a reason for happiness, happiness ensues. It is a side effect of having a purpose, of having a meaning to one's life.

Long-term happiness is a result of taking rational actions that are in accordance with universal principles. I think of happiness as the endgame of action, not because it is a state of mind for which you should consciously strive, but because happiness is an end in itself. In that vein, Aristotle appropriately described happiness as a condition rather than a destination. Happiness is a result—a symptom, as it were—of "living right." So, rather than focusing on happiness, focus on truthful, value-oriented, self-disciplined action. Such action will lead to happiness as sure as day follows night, while focusing on happiness itself is likely to yield only disappointment and frustration.

In this regard, it is important to recognize that the achievement of goals does not provide an ongoing sense of happiness. On the contrary, if one depends on ultimate triumph for his happiness, he is destined to experience a tremendous letdown after the short-term euphoria of victory wears off. Real happiness lies not in the achievement of goals, but in the striving toward goals. Striving implies action; achievement implies inertia, or an end to the action that brought about the achievement. You have to have a purpose in life that does not fade away once you achieve a goal or reach a milestone.

Many young people fall into the trap of doing something temporarily just to make money, with the intention of doing what they really want to do later on when their financial condition is more stable. Billionaire Warren Buffet put this kind of logic into proper perspective in an interview with *Fortune* magazine when he said, "I can certainly define happiness, because happy is what I am. I get to do what I like to do every single day of the year. . . . I tap-dance to work, and when I get there I'm supposed to lie on my back and paint the ceiling. It's tremendous fun. . . . They say success is getting what you want and happiness is wanting what you get. . . . I always worry about people who say, 'I'm going to do this for ten years; I really don't like it very well. And then I'll do this. . . .' That's a little like saving up sex for your old age. Not a very good idea."

EXTREME HAPPINESS

Perhaps the most action-oriented time of my life, both physically and mentally, was in my mid-twenties. Being in the men's apparel business, I spent a lot of time in New York. I was passionate about my work, and was on the go night and day. I didn't have any money to speak of, so I got to know the less trendy parts of Manhattan, Brooklyn, and Queens pretty well.

It was an exciting time—high hopes, eternal youth, and a world of opportunity. Sleep was an occasional distraction, gourmet dining was a corned beef sandwich at a Lower East Side deli. I could not have imagined a more exhilarating activity than walking around Greenwich Village, taking the subway to Sheepshead Bay in Brooklyn, or browsing at Macy's on 34th Street at a time when only New York could boast of having a Macy's store.

I usually stayed at the old Prince George Hotel on 28th Street, as it was inexpensive and more than suitable for my needs at the time. Best of all, there was an automat right across the street, and when it came to dining treats, the automat was just a notch below my favorite deli. As exciting as those times were for me, I probably did not fully appreciate the magnificence of it all. There was a feeling of urban spirituality that I certainly will never again experience—first, because I will never again be in my mid-twenties; second, because the world was much younger than today—much more innocent and wholesome.

What I now understand is that I was in a very high state of consciousness, a consciousness that would have been impossible for me to intentionally achieve. In retrospect, I realize that my hyperconscious state was a prerequisite for what was about to happen to me. One beautiful, sunny day in November, I was driving on the Grand Central Parkway on my way to JFK International Airport. My mind was exploding with a thousand and one thoughts about my life, both business and personal. Then, just as I began steering my car south onto the Van Wyke Expressway, my entire life seemed to freeze in sharp focus. It was as though I were being given the means to solve all of my business and personal problems simultaneously. It was an impossible-to-describe feeling of total control.

Instead of having to exert the usual intense mental effort to sort out my thoughts, every item that was of importance to me at the time—perhaps forty or fifty in number—instantly became clearly fixed in my mind in such an orderly fashion that I felt almost omniscient. It seemed as though a bright light had suddenly brought my thoughts out of the dark recesses of my subconscious mind and allowed me to consciously focus on all of them at once. It was a feeling of immense power, joy, and inner ecstasy.

I do not recall exactly how long that ecstatic feeling of heightened awareness lasted, but I would estimate that it was perhaps two or three minutes in length. Since that time, I have had similar experiences on a handful of occasions, each of them lasting only a matter of seconds, but nothing to match the intensity of that unexpected blink of consciousness I experienced on my way to JFK Airport. In every case, though, my heightened awareness and resulting joy came at times when my life was intensely active. Because of my experience in New York, in particular, I could relate to the heightened-state-of-awareness experiences of Dr. Richard Maurice Bucke and Harold W. Percival that I described in Chapter 1.

BY DICTIONARY DEFINITION, JOY is "an emotion of great happiness." I would be tempted to refer to it as ultimate happiness, but that would raise the same question I have with absolute happiness; i.e., there is no accurate way to quantify either happiness or joy. The truth is that none of us can ever be certain of what constitutes ultimate happiness.

It would therefore seem logical to assume that joy can vary in intensity, but I believe it always carries with it a conscious awareness of being connected to every atom in the universe. Whatever it is, joy seems to invite itself into our lives without warning. You've undoubtedly had at least one experience that you could describe as joy, a moment in time when everything seemed just perfect. Most likely, you can recall the day, and possibly even joy's moment of onset, very clearly, as well as the circumstances surrounding it.

If true joy is, in fact, just an extreme form of happiness, why does it visit us so rarely and so unexpectedly? I believe it's because you cannot anticipate joy; joy is the present. You can't plan to be joyful any more than you can plan to be happy. Keeping in mind the dangers of paradoxical intention, one must always be wary not to focus on joy itself, but, rather, on those principles that lead to joy.

It is safe to say, then, that you go about pursuing joy the same way you go about pursuing happiness, which is to say that you don't consciously pursue it at all. As many people reach their golden years, particularly people of means, they often find themselves asking the age-old question, "Is that all there is?" The probable catalyst in such cases is that there is too much focus on happiness itself rather than on those things that lead to happiness.

This is especially true of people who obsessively focus on material possessions as a means to happiness. In fact, I believe that a majority of people truly believe that making "a lot of money" would make them happy. But the will to money is just another form of the will to power, and the will to power always brings about self-destruction.

The same is true when money becomes an end in itself. When money becomes someone's chief goal, he runs the danger of becoming *possessed* by money. In truth, money and a meaningful life have very little direct connection to one another. It's certainly possible to be happy (or happier) with money, but money finds its way into your life more easily when it is a side effect of a higher purpose. In other words, more often than not, happiness is a by-product of a meaningful life.

I believe that joy, on those rare occasions when it visits us, is the result of taking constant, rational actions that are in accordance with universal principles—which includes a relentless search for, and discovery of, truth. Leonardo da Vinci hinted at this when he observed that "the noblest pleasure is the joy of understanding," which I find to be a most interesting combination of words—*pleasure, joy,* and *understanding* all in one short sentence. Understanding is a result of a successful search for truth, which da Vinci referred to as joyful, and joy equates to extreme pleasure.

I think it is safe to say that a permanent state of joy is not possible on a secular level. In fact, happiness on any level cannot be ongoing, because pain is an integral and important part of life. Pain gives us a reference point for experiencing pleasure. Ill health gives us a reference point for experiencing the pleasure of good health; poverty gives us a reference point for experiencing the pleasure of wealth; losing gives us a reference point for experiencing the pleasure of winning. Life itself would not be precious to us without the reality of death. In the words of Carl Jung, "Even a happy life cannot be without a measure of darkness, and the word *happy* would lose its meaning if it were not balanced by sadness."

To fight pain sets in motion a sort of reverse paradoxical intention; i.e., the more you focus on not experiencing pain, the less likely you are to eliminate it. For this reason, it is critically important to accept pain as a normal part of life. Think of pain as a teacher. Learn from it. Use it for personal growth. Ironically, to reduce the amount of pain in your life, it is important not to fight pain.

THE TIME IS NOW

Finally, as you make your way through life with a heightened sense of awareness, it's okay to have compassion for people who live couch-potato lives, but be sure to keep them out of *your* life. Let others live their lives as they so choose. The consequences of their actions will be *their* consequences, not yours.

If, instead, you choose to focus on achieving worthy, constructive, long-term goals, your actions not only will benefit you, but will not be harmful to anyone else. As a bonus, to the extent you are successful, you will be in a position to make constructive contributions to loved ones, and, through the wonders of the marketplace, to the world in general.

This being the case, I urge you to be bold. Venture out. Take action *now,* and refuse to allow the possibility of failure to deter you. Failure is good for the soul, good for your character, and great for learning. Whatever your age, whatever your occupation, whatever your circumstances, don't allow the fear of change to hold you back. If you wait until you have all the answers and all uncertainty has been removed, you're setting a lethal precedent for yourself. If you're suffering from adversity, that's the best reason of all for taking action. You solve problems by confronting them, not by sitting on your hands and lamenting your "bad luck."

Taking action will bring genius, magic, and power into your life. I guarantee it. And the more action you take, the more genius, magic, and power it will produce. Put them together with the aid of the Cosmic Catalyst, and you've got an unbeatable hand. Theory is good for the intellect, but action is good for the soul. It's also good for your mental health, your physical health, and your pocketbook.

Perhaps we should all heed the words of Michael Landon—producer, director, writer, and superstar—who died of pancreatic cancer in 1991, at age fifty-four, at the peak of his career. Said Landon, "Somebody should tell us, right at the start of our lives, that we are dying. Then we might live life to the limit, every minute of every day. Do it! I say. Whatever you want to do, do it now! There are only so many tomorrows."

Forget about taking action next week; forget about taking action tomorrow; forget about taking action in an hour. When you close this book, get up out of your chair and take action *now*. It's okay if you begin with a small action, but make it a constructive action. Just do it *now*. Then *keep right on taking action*—bigger and better action each step of the way—so long as you are able to breathe. To paraphrase Disraeli, action may not always bring you happiness, because your actions could be wrong. But it's a certainty that you will never find happiness without taking action.

An old Scottish proverb says, "*Be happy while you are living, for you are a long time dead.*" Procrastination is death, sedentariness is death, homeostasis is death. By contrast, the more action you take, the more expansive your mental paradigm will become and the stronger your connection to the infinite powers of the Cosmic Catalyst will be.

Action is life—and life is meant to be lived.

Robert Ringer is an American icon whose insights into life have helped more people transform their aspirations and goals into reality than perhaps any other author in history. For more than three decades, his works have stood alone as the gospel when it comes to conveying worldly wisdom to millions of readers worldwide.

He is the author of two *New York Times* #1 bestsellers, both of which have been listed by *The New York Times* among the 15 best-selling motivational books of all time. He is also the publisher of RobertRinger.com, where he combines philosophy, reality, and action in his trademark style that translates into tangible results for his readers.

Ringer has appeared on numerous national television and radio shows, including *The Tonight Show, Today, The Dennis Miller Show, Good Morning America, ABC Nightline, The Charlie Rose Show,* and has made a variety of appearances on Fox News and Fox Business.

He also has been the subject of feature articles in such major publications as *Time, People, The Wall Street Journal, Fortune, Barron's,* and *The New York Times.*

To learn about Robert Ringer's life-changing new program, *Fast Track to Dealmaking Fortunes,* visit http://robertringer.com/action.